Disappeared for Good

A Memoir of Finding God's Goodness
in the Midst of Trauma

⚜

JEANNE GRIENER

Disappeared for Good:
A Memoir of Finding God's Goodness in the Midst of Trauma

Copyright © 2021 by Jeanne Griener. All Rights Reserved.

Publisher: Red Tulip Media, LLC, Kansas City, MO.

Scripture quotations taken from the (NASB®) New American Standard Bible®, Copyright 2020 by The Lockman Foundation. Used by permission. All rights reserved. www.lockman.org.

Scripture taken from the Holy Bible, New International Version®, NIV®. Copyright ©1973, 1978,1984, 2011 by Biblica, Inc.™ Used by permission of Zondervan. All rights reserved worldwide. www.zondervan.com. The "NIV" and "New International Version" are trademarks registered in the United States Patent and Trademark Office by Biblica, Inc.™

Scripture taken from the New King James Version®. Copyright © 1982 by Thomas Nelson. Used by permission. All rights reserved.

Scripture taken from the Revised Standard Version of the Bible, copyright © 1946, 1952, and 1971. The Division of Christian Education of the National Council of the Church of Christ in the United States of America. Used by permission. All rights reserved.

All Internet addresses presented in this book are offered as a resource. They are not intended in any way to be or imply an endorsement by the author, nor does the author vouch for the content of these sites for the life of this book.

NOTE: This is a creative nonfictional account of my traumatic life experiences. This is my story—my memory of events and my perceptions. With any memory, it has flaws. I did not remember word-for-word the conversations represented here, but the gist and purpose of the conversations are correct. Like witnesses to an accident, others may remember the situations differently. Where possible, I used actual public records. If I got the situation wrong, I apologize, but I believe in the truthfulness of my memoir. This is what I remember. This is what I experienced.

Please also note that while I love God's Word, I am not a theologian.

ISBN is 979-8-9854786-0-0

Author's photo by Justin Cunningham

DEDICATION

I dedicate this book to the sweet memories of my brother, Richard; my father, Merle, who taught me to love beauty and to serve others; my mother, Helen, who loved and nurtured her family well; my son, Daniel, who inspires me daily and encouraged me to write this; Randy, my husband, whose gentleness is a refuge in the sad moments; Robin, who has traveled with me through the entire journey—you are a Treasure from our Father; and Jesus Christ, my Savior and Lord, who is giving me Life abundantly. Each of you has enriched my life and I am so thankful for you. I love you.

CONTENTS

Introduction ... 1
1. Rumblings ... 5
2. Disappearance ... 13
3. Terror ... 23
4. Chaos ... 31
5. Normalcy ... 51
6. Yearning ... 73
7. Forgiveness ... 79
8. Mountains ... 89
9. Goodness ... 97
Prayer for Readers ... 105
Notes ... 107
Acknowledgments ... 110
Postscript ... 111

"And we know that God causes all things to work together for good to those who love God, to those who are called according to His purpose."
Romans 8:28, NASB

INTRODUCTION

And he [God] passed in front of Moses, proclaiming, "The LORD, the LORD, the compassionate and gracious God, slow to anger, abounding in love and faithfulness, maintaining love to thousands, and forgiving wickedness, rebellion and sin. Yet He does not leave the guilty unpunished....

—Exodus 34:6-7 (NIV)

The trauma began on an endless night in 1972. Appalling distress and shattered hope became the norm to my close-knit family. I rarely spoke of the terrific loss that wreaked havoc on us in central Illinois. How could I?

How was I to express the cruelty and pain? It was too bizarre to articulate; too incomprehensible for others, let alone my eleven-year-self, to understand. The horrific event was too inconceivable to process, yet my family and I lived it. I sought relative safety by not expressing the suffering nor articulating the void of the unknown.

* * *

I have always been drawn by quiet like a butterfly to a fragrant pink blossom. I naturally seek restful places, like my garden. Listening to the birdsong and the drone of bees comforts me. The zip of a hummingbird is a treasured moment. Pondering the flight of a bumblebee inspires me. I slip away to the garden daily anticipating the soon-to-be-open bloom. It is enthralling to witness the subtly of growth, noting the day-to-day changes in the bud. When it opens I am captivated by its beauty and intricacies! The quiet of the garden grounds me. There I am refreshed and connected with God the Father.

I cannot remember a time I did not know God as a loving Creator. In my fourth spring, I squatted in front of my first tulip and brushed off the early snow. As I studied the beauty of the black center filled with yellow stamens, all surrounded by deep red petals, I sensed Him there with me. Peace blanketed me as I thanked God for the beauty of this bloom. He smiled back at me through that red tulip.

In quiet, there was safety and peace. Horrors and unknowns did not belong there. Violence and tragedy had no place in the quiet. At least, I believed that in my early years.

My beloved thirteen-year-old brother, Richard, disappeared. The horror my family faced was not just that he vanished without a trace, but the subsequent living with no answers, no help, no advocates, no clues, and no finality. Endlessly....

I retreated inwards, yearning for answers, hoping for comfort... None came.

Yet strength grew. An awareness of others' suffering terror and injustice stirred within me. Along with that, became an awareness of something pure, just, and strong. The faith I had as a very young child blossomed in me as I healed from the trauma.

Sometimes there are no answers from humankind. However, Jesus is alive and active. He met me in my cave of safe solitude. Then He wooed me to the mountaintop to proclaim freedom to other captives! He shouted to my heart, "Tell your story! Bring My Hope to others!"

This is my small portion of understanding God's Goodness in the midst of tragedy and trauma. Along my journey I have experienced fear, anger, shame, and brokenness. Yet, I have also been faithful, peaceful, and hopeful.

Jesus always met me with Compassion and Mercy. He helped me persevere. His Truth set me free. He gave me His answers and I now comprehend His Justice.

Journey with me on the path of God's Goodness. He will never falter or fail.

God's Love never fails.

1

Rumblings

December 1971–January 16, 1972

And the God of peace will crush Satan under your feet shortly. The grace of our Lord Jesus Christ be with you. Amen.
—Romans 16:20 (NKJV)

In 1971, Pekin, Illinois, was like most Midwestern working-class cities of about thirty-one thousand. The area was energized by light to heavy industry and agriculture. Most worker bees lived in middle-class homes like ours and droned through the days. The town was bordered by the heavily traveled Illinois River to the west. The ever-busy Peoria & Pekin Union Railroad sliced the city in half. At its eastern border, the prairies spread out—an endless expanse of grain and sky. Pekin, itself, however, boasted a few steep hills that hid caves left over from old coal mining. In the winter, the natural Mineral Springs Lagoon iced over, drawing out colorfully garbed children who skated grooves in the thick ice amid challenges of "Betcha can't do this!"

Being the typical pesky sister, I always tagged along with my big brother, Richard, and his friends. I wanted to do everything he did.

However, that day Richard and his friends zoomed past me on the ice as they raced from one end of the lagoon to the other.

I loved winter. The snow and ice meant winter fun. But the best part was Christmas. I loved the smell of baking sweet treats, the sight of the twinkling tinsel on the tree, the singing of carols with my mom, and Dad reading about Jesus's birth in a stable. Every year I vied with my brother for who lit the final, red Advent candle. He usually did it because he was older.

Just once *I* wanted to light it.

Traditions, gentle and comfortable, warmed me. My hopes shone like the star at the top of the evergreen in our living room. My favorite tradition, though, was gift giving. Or for my selfish self, gift receiving.

This year I was confident the anticipation would kill me! Two days before Christmas, my brother tramped down the basement steps as Mom stood in front of the closed door. She patted my cheek. "Stay out of the basement, young lady, or you'll ruin the surprise." Richard had been given permission to work in the basement on a gift for me. For me! I spun in circles!

The basement held my father's massive workbench. He was a master wood craftsman and had taught both of us children to use his tools. Richard was proficient at it. I preferred to watch the two of them working.

Later that day, I pressed my ear against the closed basement door while Mom was in another room. I expected to hear sawing and hammering. Instead, I heard nothing. Not even a dropped nail. What was Richard making me?

That night, I lay in the still house with my eyes and ears on high alert. When I thought everyone was sleeping, I slipped out of my room and crept to the basement. I sneaked open the door and slunk down the dark staircase. When my bare foot touched the basement floor, a groan filled the room as the furnace kicked on. The furnace monster was loose! I raced back to my comfortable bed.

The next day, Christmas Eve, my grandmother arrived from southern Illinois with her trunk loaded with glittering packages and tins of sweet gooies. As Grandmother bent to receive a greeting hug, I kept one eye on the goods in the trunk. My brother and I unloaded and unloaded and unloaded the Christmas cache, giving each box a curious shake. Our house overflowed with all the fun of Christmas.

That night, Grandmother took my bed, so I lay on the floor of Richard's room. I peppered him with questions about what he had made me.

"Is it bigger than a hat box?"

He played along, smiling at me. "Yes."

"Is it heavy?"

"No."

"Is it something I can sit on?"

He wrinkled his face. "No."

"Is it something I can wear?"

"No, silly!" He laughed.

He had made a child-powered go-cart last summer that all of us neighborhood children enjoyed. "Does it have wheels?"

"No!" He looked so smug I threw my pillow in his face.

Richard was just as resolved not to tell me about his gift, as I was to find out. Then he started telling me puns and riddles. We laughed late into the night until our father boomed out for us to be still. We snickered at that too. I finally drifted off to sleep, warmth from my brother's love comforting me.

The next morning, a huge dollhouse made of cardboard sat

beside the Christmas tree. *This* is what my brother had made for me. He explained it might be too heavy for me if he had made it out of wood. My gratitude erupted in a tight squeeze around Richard's waist. He smiled down at me then wriggled away. Enough of that!

Grandmother's gifts were socks, books, a nice piece of jewelry, and a few dollars for us each. I received an empty locket designed to hold tiny photographs. Richard received a new watch.

It was a good Christmas, filled with gifts, treats, and love.

After Grandmother left the next day, Mom and Dad reminded us of our manners. They insisted that we write a thank-you to our grandmother for her gifts. I was happy about filling the locket she had given me with pictures of my family. I also thanked her for the money because I was excited about purchasing a paint-by-number kit.

It was now time to plead. "Mom, can you drive us Arlan's Department Store? I need to spend my Christmas money." I had already set my sights on a canvas of three kittens, whose big eyes called to me, "Bring us home."

Richard nodded. "Yeah, Mom, I want to buy a new toy train engine." Dad and Richard had converted the Ping-Pong table into an extensive layout with tracks, hills, bridges, and tunnels.

Later that week we drove to Arlan's Department Store. I snatched up the new paint-by-number set, but Richard walked through the toy section empty-handed. The store did not carry the specific engine he wanted. I trailed behind him as he again scanned the aisles of bright new toys. Eager to help, I suggested he purchase the Hot Wheels there on the shelf. Awed with his ability to leave without a single package in his hands, I told him he could help me paint. He was so much wiser than I.

After we arrived back home, our mother helped Richard order a specific toy engine at a nearby hobby store. The storeowner told

Mom he would call when the new engine arrived, and we could pick it up.

It was a cold and overcast day on Friday, January 14, when we loaded into the car to travel to Peoria, Illinois, a neighboring large city. The Signal House Hobby Store was an open room with several makeshift tables loaded with model train cars, engines, and train set paraphernalia. Besides the manager, there was only one other person present—a large, gray-haired man who appeared unkempt in his black drover's coat and heavy boots. He did not seem to be buying anything. He was walking up and down the rows of displayed toy trains, laughing to himself.

Richard went right to shopping, while Mom turned her back to him to talk to the manager. I leaned against the counter, watching the large, strange customer. The man did not pick up any toy engine or train car. He did not look at any item for sale.

His eyes were fixed on my brother.

Our strict parents had taught us to be mannerly to others, especially adults. We did not initiate conversations with them—a restriction that came naturally since both my brother and I were shy and reserved. But something about this man....

Narrowing my eyes, I scrutinized the interaction between him and my brother. The man was talking to Richard. They stood about four feet apart, facing one another. Then man took a deep breath and bent a bit backward, bellowing out an amazingly realistic sound of a freight train whistle!

"*To-oo-oo-t!*"

Richard stood spellbound! The man straightened, towered over Richard, and snickered.

I had never seen my brother so engrossed in another person. It did not add up in my brain—a grown man more interested in my brother than the toy trains, and my brother more interested in the odd man than his own special purchase? Such behavior poured anxiety into my heart.

I tugged on our mother's coat. She had to intervene!

Mom shushed me for interrupting. Yet I sensed deep in my heart something was not right.

Richard had to get away from that man.

My heart impelled me to plant myself between the stranger and my brother. I addressed Richard, but faced the man and shouted, "Stay away from that man! That man is evil!"

The man sneered at me and made a threatening step toward me. Deep inside I shivered, but I did not move. I kept my eyes locked on him.

I was not a dramatic child. I did not have flights of fancy, nor did I get so lost in my imagination that I was out of touch with the here and now. And I certainly did not make a practice of yelling at adults. But I had to make others aware of the danger I perceived.

The commotion caused both our mother and the manager to rush over, attempting to calm everyone. The manager raised one eyebrow toward the bedraggled man while my mother gathered us close. Richard seemed to realize it was time to leave. I continued to be guarded, observing everyone.

Well! It did not turn out as I had hoped. No one else discerned any danger to my brother. Instead, Mom yanked my arm and hissed, "What has gotten into you? That was rude! You know better than that, young lady."

Mom nodded to the rough-looking customer. Then she turned to the manager. "I am so sorry about my daughter's outburst. That is just not like her. I assure you she knows better." She then aimed her gaze at my brother. "Richard, it's time to leave. Now."

With one hand still on my arm, she eyed the exit. Richard paid for his new train engine, but craned his head backward toward the odd man as we left the store.

At the car, my mother glared at me. "Can you explain that rude behavior? That was awful!"

I could not. How could Mom and Richard not perceive a danger that was so clear to me? Why could they not understand? Could they not fathom the evil emanating from the large man?

I did not know how to articulate to my family what I perceived. All my life, I had sensed unseen attributes about others, but this was the first time I experienced such an intense wickedness. I just *knew* that Richard had to get away from that man! It seemed inherent to me to grasp the invisible, and to comprehend situations with more than my natural senses. This astuteness was an odd and enigmatic insight—a knowing. Unexplainable. Yet the danger I'd felt was as real to me as the cold, hard seat and the gray clouds overhead.

I was still concerned that Richard was so engrossed by the rough man's unique whistle; he was trying to imitate it as we drove home. It was uncanny.

I rode home unsettled, yet silent. I understood why Mom scolded me. I was old enough and polite enough not to confront an adult, especially to say that he was evil. Normally, even *I* would consider it excessive and rude behavior. This situation, however, disturbed me.

I had discerned. I had acted. I had spoken against that which I sensed.

It was not enough.

2

Disappearance

JANUARY 17, 1972

You are my hiding place; You shall preserve me from trouble; You shall surround me with songs of deliverance.

—Psalm 32:7 (NKJV)

January 17, 1972, was a mundane Monday (Dr. Martin Luther King, Jr.'s birthday was not yet a national holiday). Our family prepared for the usual requirements of the day: work and school.

Dad was a skilled craftsman with formal training as a patternmaker. He built wooden molds for items that would then be cast in molten metals or plastics. He made patterns for a great variety of items, from small lawn sprinklers to huge turbines. Dad had just opened his own shop as a freelancer working evenings and weekends. To make ends meet, he worked construction at a power plant during the week. That Monday, he dressed in multiple layers and took two thermoses of coffee with him to stay warm. It was dark outside when he left and it would be dark when he arrived home around 5:30 PM.

Mom was a registered nurse who worked at the local hospital day shift. She had to be on the floor for a 7:00 AM shift change. She woke Richard and me before leaving the house. She had our breakfasts fixed and helped us pack our lunches. She would be home when we came back from school. Mom reminded me that today was Girl Scouts day, so I should wear my uniform. I had a meeting in a neighbor's basement until 5:00 PM.

Just like every mundane Monday.

Two things, however, set this Monday apart. First, the day before, Richard had purchased a bright blue Coleco Slide-A-Boggan—a slick piece of plastic that could be rolled up to carry and unrolled to zip across the snow. Second, this cold January Monday glistened with white crystals. Perfect for sledding!

When I returned from the Girl Scouts' meeting, my brother wasn't home. That was unusual. I asked Mom where he was, and she explained that he had asked to go sledding to try out his new purchase. Though he asked some friends to join him, they all had other plans so he promised to be careful. Mom agreed Richard could walk to the sledding hill, but he was to be home at 5:30. To ensure he was prompt, Richard wore his new watch.

Richard was obedient. Our parents never had to tell him anything twice.

Our favorite sledding hill, situated one mile from our modest ranch house, was one of two campuses of our local high school. The school itself sat upon the hill, making it a proud landmark in the community. Yet Richard and I were more interested in the hill itself. It was open and steep, with only a quiet road ambling at the base.

Richard had to be there.

Mom was fixing dinner, and I began to set the table, as was our routine. Mom looked at the clock and her brow furrowed. "Richard should be home any minute."

He was probably outside lobbing snowballs at his friends under the glow of the streetlights. I sneaked a peek out the front window. He wasn't there.

I cast furtive glances at the clock as I finished setting the table. I didn't say anything to Mom, but Richard was late. I had never known my brother to be late for anything.

Dad arrived home, welcomed by the savory aromas coming from the cooking pots that made me aware of how hungry I was. I gave him a hug, and he greeted Mom with a peck.

"Where's Richard?"

I watched as he looked intently into Mom's eyes. I could see the concern on her face.

"He's not home yet. I told him to be home at 5:30. I don't know where he could be. I'm worried." Mom knotted her apron, eyes focused on the clock instead of Dad.

Without undressing from his heavy winter gear, Dad hurried to turn on the garage floodlights and then the front porch light. He stepped onto the front stoop and frowned. Then he whistled into the cold night air.

Years earlier, when Dad believed we were old enough to leave the yard, he held our hands and whistled like that. It was so loud and piercing that it lifted the hair on my arms! Smiling, he explained, "When you hear that sound, it's time to come home. I will only whistle once, so you have to be listening for it." From that day forward, whenever we left the yard we kept one ear open for Dad's come-home-now whistle. When we heard that shrill sound, we'd grab our gear and race for home.

Dad whistled again. Surely, Richard would race around the corner at that sound!

He didn't.

Mom had turned off the stove, supper forgotten. She joined Dad on the front stoop, placing her hand on his shoulder, her brow knitted together.

I huddled by the front living room window, hugging myself, searching my parents' faces. They knew what needed to be done. I strained to hear Richard shouting a response. Instead, the only sound was the eerie call of a freight train.

Where was my brother?

After Dad's third whistle, he turned to face my mother. He looked straight into her eyes and took her hand. "I don't like this. I think I should go look for Richard. He may be injured. I'm going to drive to the sledding hill and look for him on foot."

"I want to help, Dad."

A look passed between Dad and Mom. Then he nodded and looked at me. "All right, but hurry. I'm not going to wait long for you to get ready. I want to get going right away."

I dashed into the mudroom, pulling on my bulky warm clothes.

Dad and I drove to the parking lot across from the sledding hill in silence. He reached over and squeezed my shoulder. That steadied my heart as I sat forward in my seat, straining to see in the dark.

Once parked at the base of the hill, we grabbed flashlights. Mitten to mitten, I held my dad's hand as we tromped through the snow. Dad swept the beam of a heavy flashlight over the bumps of the sledding hill. I followed his example, calling out my brother's name and then listening to the silence. Fear, more than snow, weighed down my legs.

All we saw was packed snow and trees. We walked around every perimeter tree, still calling his name. We neared a copse of trees on the north side of the hill, across the street from the railroad tracks.

Suddenly terrified, I couldn't look around the huge cottonwood trunk alone. It wasn't rational; it was just what I felt.

Dad seemed to sense my unease and took my hand again. Then we continued our search. We neither saw nor heard anything. No sled, no gloves, no hat...

No Richard.

Dad stopped and listened again. The winter night held no sounds. He shouted into the bitter cold air with all his might. "Richard! Son! It's Dad. I need to know you are safe. Let me know where you are. I love you, son!"

We stood still for a minute, listening. Only our steamy breath answered us.

I tugged on my dad's heavy coat. "Dad, sometimes Richard and I don't walk to here on the sidewalks. Sometimes we cross Broadway Street and cut through the railroad yard." Taking this dangerous shortcut would usually earn us a scolding or cause us to be grounded for a week. That seemed mild compared to the knots now in my stomach.

We walked across the street into the railroad right of way. There were a few boxcars further west of where we stood. It was not uncommon for open and empty cars to sit idle on these tracks.

As we stood on the first track, Dad swung his light beam back and forth across the area. It was a tangle of old ties, dead weeds, and snow-covered trash. Nothing compelled Dad to look further at that moment because he covered my mittened hand with his own and said, "Let's go back home to check on Mom. I bet Richard made it there and we simply missed each other."

We returned to the vehicle without our beloved son and brother. Creeping along toward home, Dad stretched his head out the open window, straining to see or hear anything leading to Richard. He instructed me to keep my eyes on my side of the road as he did the same on his side. Sometimes he called out Richard's name. We looked in ditches and in people's front yards.

There was no sign of my brother.

When we arrived home, Mom was beside herself, eaten up with worry. She paced and repeatedly scrunched her apron with her hands. "Merle, he isn't here! Where is he? Why isn't he home? He promised me he would be home by now. Something awful has happened, I just know it."

"Hon, it'll be okay. Jeanne and I will go back out. We must have just crossed paths. He will be home any minute now." The taut lines on his forehead belied his words.

By the time we returned from our second futile search for Richard, it was almost 6:30. My mother's face pinched. Dad looked troubled, but remained calm. As for me?

Anxiety built a nest in my gut.

Dad placed both hands on Mom's shoulder. "Helen, I think we need to call the police to help us. I don't know what else to do."

Mom gave a shaky nod. I held my breath as she picked up the phone. "This is Mrs. Merle Griener. We need help finding our son. He went sledding and now he's an hour late. Officer, this is just not like him."

She sputtered her concern into the phone. "He suffered blackouts and a coma last year. I'm concerned that may have happened again." She listened for a moment, and then nodded. "Thank you."

When she hung up she relayed back to us the police were sending a squad car to patrol the route Richard walked from the junior high to the sledding hill, including the area around the railroad tracks.

I exhaled relief. Dad and Mom hugged.

At that time, police protocol did not distinguish between a

missing child and a missing adult. The police had to wait twenty-four hours before initiating a search. However, because of my brother's medical past, the police patrol car began their search at 6:30 PM.

Still in my outerwear, I was determined not to let my parents out of my sight. We were fighting to find Richard! I stayed close and listened, ready to jump into action if one of my parents asked. Yet, we just stood still in the kitchen.

Mom rubbed her own arms as if to remove the chill. "What's next? What do we do? Oh, Merle. I am scared."

"I know, Helen. Me, too. But we'll find him. Call the neighbors. Maybe he stopped to warm up at one of their houses. Somebody has to know something. I'm going to stop by a friend's house and together we'll go look again. I will check back in an hour." He kissed Mom on the cheek.

Then he turned to me and kissed me on the top of my head, "Jeanne, stay with your mother."

I stripped out of my heavy winter wear, as frightful speculations ran through my mind unhindered. Where was Richard? Was he harmed or injured? Had he fallen suddenly ill? Was he conscious? Why couldn't we find him?

My little heart could only absorb so much confusion. Baffling and intense memories of the trip to the hobby store were lost under layers of dread. Disquiet, like a riptide, dragged me away from clarity.

Years later, it mattered that I didn't remember. Years later, it mattered that Mom, too, didn't remember.

But that night, I stood near my mom, comforted by her closeness, as she started calling friends and neighbors who then soon filled the house, bringing with them sandwiches and coffee. I wandered unnoticed between the crowded kitchen and living room, unable to find quiet. I couldn't sit still. Looping through the rooms of the house seemed to offer a false sense of ease.

By 8:00 PM the house was a bevy of activity. Men garbed in duck-cloth coveralls and heavy boots were gathering outside in the garage preparing to go on organized searches, while some ladies filled plates with cold sandwiches and brewed huge pots of coffee. I had just settled onto the sofa, listening to the women talk in hushed tones, when the front doorbell rang.

With Mom beside me, I opened the door to a uniformed police officer. He asked to do a search of the house. He breezed past me, commenting that Richard was probably just hiding. Having never seen an armed police officer up close, I followed him as he walked to Richard's bedroom and peered under the dust ruffle. As he opened Richard's closet door, I told the officer, "He's not in there. I've already searched. I've looked in every hiding spot we have. He's not here."

The officer brushed past me as if I were a dust mite. We had already searched in every spot of the house. Yet, the police officer looked throughout the house, the garage, and the yard. Then he interviewed my mother.

Mom reiterated that Richard was a responsible and prompt child. She repeated that he had been in a coma the previous autumn due to an acute case of encephalitis, and she was concerned that had flared again. Upon hearing this, the police called another squad car in on the search and asked auxiliary members to join them. The patrol officer also explained the police planned to ask Civil Defense to help. They would notify the chief if Richard had not returned by 9:00 PM.

In one hour.

I drifted into the kitchen, listening. Even though I had not eaten supper, the sandwiches seemed offensive to my nose. I stood under the clock, watching the minute hand move. Nine o'clock came without any news.

Dad had just returned from searching to grab a warm cup of coffee when there was another knock. But this time it was on the back door. I hovered close to Dad as he placed one hand on my shoulder and opened the door with the other. The bright floodlights on the backdoor illuminated a small band of unknown men and boys. All were dressed in winter outdoor gear.

Afraid and curious, I stood still next to Dad.

The first man looked into Dad's eyes. "We heard about your son from a ham-radio operator. We have come to help. We have sons too."

My dad teared up and covered his eyes with his right hand. When his shoulders stopped shaking, he invited the small band of volunteers to follow him into the garage.

The strangers offering to help intrigued me. At a time when my brother and I were usually tucked into bed, I could see boys my brother's age standing behind their fathers, their breath visible in the cold. These strangers left the warmth of their homes to aid us! I had never experienced such kindness from strangers.

In the garage, Dad, some of his friends, and now these volunteer searchers turned sawhorses and plywood into makeshift tables. Someone had a detailed map of Pekin they were using to organize the searches. Then the men left in groups, each assigned to different areas. A couple of neighbors stayed behind to administrate the search.

I wandered back into the house and went to my room to escape the confusion. I sat on my bed in the dark room and wept. Where was my brother? Was Richard harmed? Why would anyone harm him? Why couldn't the adults I trusted find him? Would he survive the cold this night? How did someone disappear like this? Why?

I couldn't sleep. Guilt for being in the warm house mocked my rest. My brother was alone in the bitter winter cold. Yet, the busyness within the house drew me back and I wandered into the kitchen. All night, like a mouse peeking from a peephole, I watched as people came and went.

No one stopped; no one slept.

The night was endless.

3

Terror

JANUARY 18, 1972

In righteousness you shall be established;
You shall be far from oppression, for you shall not fear;
And from terror, for it shall not come near you.

—Isaiah 54:14 (NKJV)

*P*ekin Police were now officially in charge of the search as the Civil Defense supported the officers by providing gridded maps and by organizing volunteers. Search headquarters were established in the upper room of Memorial Arena, across the street from both the sledding hill and the railroad tracks. The ice rink where Richard and I had often zipped around laughing now opened its doors to searchers needing rest, warm food and beverages, all donated by local businesses.

The police stayed active all through the early morning hours of January 18th. They had dispatched a description of Richard to other agencies through a Law Enforcement Enquiry Department (LEED) notification. Additionally, a local radio station, WSIV, was broadcasting my brother's description to listeners.

Early in the morning of January 18th there still were no signs of Richard. I must have fallen asleep sometime in the wee morning hours because I awoke before dawn in my bed, dressed in my pajamas. Every limb felt heavy. I couldn't think clearly. My heart was numb. I dragged myself into the kitchen to join my parents.

At 6:30 in the morning there was a knock. Bleary-eyed and gruff, Dad swung open the front door while Mom rushed in from the kitchen. I tailed behind and plunked on the sofa, too weary to move beyond that. A patrol officer stood on the stoop. Dad opened the door wider to allow him inside.

Had the officer brought news of Richard?

Dad's words tumbled on top of one another. "Have you found him? Do you know where our son is?"

Looking at his shoes, the officer swung his head side to side. "No, Sir." Then he raised his eyes to focus on Dad. "I don't have any news to report to you. I was wondering if we could have a pair of Richard's slippers? You see, we have a psychic in the car with us. She thought if she could just touch something of his, she would be able to help us track his whereabouts."

Dad and Mom exchanged a deep look. Dad tilted his chin to the right and bit his lower lip.

Mom's eyes were wide and her lips pursed. She looked straight into Dad's eyes. "I don't know. I don't really believe in that."

"What can it hurt, Helen? Anything is better than nothing. Let's do it."

"I don't know, Merle. I am not comfortable with it." My mom's face contorted like she had sucked a lemon. What was wrong with her?

I had never heard of a *psychic* before. Why didn't Mom believe in *that*? What was *it*? However, I knew to save my questions for when I was alone with her.

Dad set his jaw. "I think we should do it."

Mom nodded and looked at her feet, then tightened the belt on her robe and strode into Richard's room. In a few minutes she returned, holding out a pair of his slippers. She kept her eyes on the slippers as she handed them over to the patrolman.

The patrolman accepted them, then swept open the door, letting cold air fill the room.

After he left, I jumped up and squeezed my Mom around her tiny waist. I needed her closeness. Tears rolled down my cheeks as Dad's strong arms enclosed us both. We stood still, comforted by one another.

We all wandered back into the kitchen and I glided into my chair at the table. Too tired to think, I slid my elbow on the table and laid my head on it. Dad poured himself coffee and then turned on the radio. Local news and weather reports mumbled in the background as he leaned against the counter, grim and staring into space.

Mom opened the refrigerator, as was her habit every day of her life. She gazed at its contents. Finally she pulled out a carton of eggs and set them on the stove harder than usual. Then she whirled around. "Oh! Where is Richard? What do we do? I don't know what to do! I just don't know what to do." Her shoulders shook as she buried her face in her hands.

Dad embraced her. They held one another as tears flowed. He kissed the top of her head, but didn't offer any words. I stayed at my place at the table, wetting it with my tears.

I, too, had no words.

After a while, all the tears stopped. Mom fixed us eggs and toast, but it was tasteless.

Unlike our hope, dawn came bright.

After putting my dirty dishes in the sink, I stood next to where

Mom sat, looking her straight in the eyes. "Please let me stay home. I want to search for Richard! Please."

Mom looked to Dad and he nodded in agreement.

Then Dad dressed warmly and told us he was going back to search. "Helen, you and Jeanne stay here to handle any phone calls. I'll call at noon. The police will know how to find me if you need me before that."

"I want to go with you, Dad!"

"No, it's safer if you stay here with your mother."

I didn't understand nor agree; yet I obeyed.

After he left, I asked Mom about the psychic. She explained that some people sensed or saw things that weren't obvious to the natural senses. They know things others did not.

"What's wrong with it? Why don't you believe in it?"

"The Bible warns us against participating in such activity. God describes the practice as evil. I agreed to use her to honor your dad. I do not believe she will find Richard because I don't believe she has any special power."

I was left to ponder that later.

Soon the house filled with neighbors, all clamoring for information about Richard. I wandered about the house, lost between clumps of chattering women in different rooms. My heart thumped. I wasn't doing any good here. This was a waste of time!

One friend asked my mom, "Helen, do you think Richard had an accident? Do you think he is in a ditch somewhere?"

"Do you think someone hit him with his car and drove off?" Another neighbor speculated.

Yet another friend offered her thoughts: "Maybe someone found him injured on the sledding hill. Maybe he hit is head and lost his memory."

"Yes." Mom spoke in a soft voice, her brows drawn tight. "Merle and I think someone may have hit Richard with their car while he walked home. We think the driver might have taken him last night to his own house. We hope the radio announcements will encourage whomever it is to bring Richard home. I don't know what to think really. It's just so odd." Her voice trailed off as she knotted the tissue in her hands.

Their conjectures were mine. But somehow, hearing them spoken aloud felt like needles poking at my already tenuous peace. Tears flowed down my cheeks.

I walked over to my mom. She wrapped her arm around my waist. Then she blotted at her own wet eyes with a fresh tissue.

She looked into my eyes. "Jeanne, you look so tired. You have dark circles under your eyes. I know you didn't sleep much last night. Why don't you go lie down? I will wake you if we hear anything."

I was jumbled inside. "I can't sleep here. It's too noisy. And I'm afraid, Mom."

"I know, dear. I know." Mom squeezed me until my tears stopped. Again.

A neighbor touched Mom's arm. "She could nap at my house." She looked at me. "You can go to the sofa in the basement. It's quiet and dark down there."

I didn't want to leave my mom's side. Yet fatigue made my muscles leaden. A short nap, perhaps….

After Mom reassured me she would call the neighbor if she had any news, I followed the woman across the street and down to her basement. She offered me a pillow and an afghan. She turned on a small lamp and told her young children to play quietly nearby.

With tears rolling down my face, I sat on the sofa, hoping to be alone with my thoughts. However, the girls asked me to play with them. I wiped away my tears and tried to play pretend tea party, but I could only focus on finding my brother. The earlier speculations replayed in my head. After an hour of relentless agitation, I walked home.

When I arrived, the once-quiet house was a center of upheaval. The phone rang incessantly. Friends, reporters, and the police came in and out the door. In all that chaos, nothing helpful emerged: no answers, no evidence, no clues...

And no Richard.

Late in the afternoon, Mom's closest friend arrived, explaining she had come from the police station. The night before, she had been manning our home telephone. She described to us how, around 10 PM, she received a call in which a young male voice stated, "You'll never see your son alive again." She'd hung up with fright, and, not wanting to upset my parents, remained quiet about it until now.

The police responded by teaching her how to request a trace be put on a call.

I was shaken. Did we lose a vital clue by her silence?

Later that day, the police interviewed Richard's friends and teachers. A couple of neighborhood girls said Richard had playfully lobbed snowballs at them. Then he asked a few friends if they could go sledding together, but the others were busy. Richard was the only one with a free evening. His teachers disclosed he was a polite and intelligent student. No one recounted anything out of the ordinary concerning Richard's demeanor or conversations. [1,2]

I had always read the evening version of the *Pekin Daily Times* newspaper. However, on this evening's front page, my beloved brother's image smiled back at me as the headline—"Pekin Boy, 13, Still Missing"—declared my heartache. [3]

The evening news reported that a fresh sea of volunteers had resumed searching at dawn of that day, hopeful the sunlight would lead them to Richard. A local construction company donated the use of their helicopter to aid in the search. Airplanes from the Illinois State Police and the local Air National Guard branch flew over the terrain. Also, they used their jeeps and motorcycles to cover frozen ground. In addition to civilian volunteers, the Illinois State Police, the Civil Air Patrol, the Illinois Air National Guard, the Civil Defense unit, the Tazewell County Sheriff's deputies, Pekin firefighters, and Explorer Scout troops all joined in the search for my brother. The number of volunteers, with counts ranging from three to five hundred people, was nothing short of amazing. [4,5]

The sheer number of searchers touched my heart. In addition to those volunteers, local businesses donated food and beverages. With overwhelming kindness, the community generously helped to find Richard. People cared.

Simultaneously, with that many people searching and no clues found, my heart skipped beats. I squeezed my eyes to block out the sorrow. The expectation of finding Richard, or a least a clue, remained unmet.

At the close of the first day, shock, fear, and sorrow mixed in a terrifying concoction. I was nauseous. My pretty mom looked stricken. My laughing dad was now despairing. I wanted to see my parents happy. I wanted the former quiet and safety of our family. I wanted the police to make it right.

I wanted my brother home!

4

Chaos

January 19, 1972 to January 17, 1973

For God is not the author of confusion but of peace....
—I Cor. 14:33 (NJKV)

The days after Richard disappeared blurred together into a sickening slurry of events and emotions. I had trouble concentrating and sleeping. I didn't want to eat. I didn't want to play with friends. When I was overwhelmed I hid away in my closet. The act of closing the doors was like closing out the confusion, uncertainty, and fear.

And yet, the mundane tasks of life continued. After spending only one day at home, I walked to my best friend's house. From there we would walk to school together. My friend's mother greeted me at the door.

"Oh, Sweetheart!" She pulled me inside and held me. I could feel her shaking as I sobbed against her soft belly. She invited me into the kitchen to wait for my friend, and then cocked her head to one side as she watched me. She quietly reached out her right hand to click off the news coming from the radio. When my friend came in the room, she looked me straight in the eyes, squeezed my hand, and hugged me. We cried together. Her mom came over and embraced us both. We all stood in a tight circle unable to express any words for the feelings we shared.

So began another emotionally tumultuous day.

At school, aware of my classmates' stares, I wanted to run home. Before class, we stripped off our heavy winter gear and hung it in cubbies in an oversized coat closet. Some of my friends asked about my brother. Other classmates looked away from my face. I lagged behind, seeking peace, until our strict teacher called my name. She seemed dour and displeased with all of us, making me feel even more unsettled. I didn't want to be there!

After roll call, I asked permission to use the restroom, where I cried in the stall until the teacher sent someone to bring me back to class.

I could not concentrate. I picked up my pencil, but only succeeded in staring out the vast windows, silently praying someone would find my brother. I daydreamed he would be home when I arrived there. My chest hurt and I was nauseous. The only saving grace was that my closest friend was in the class with me. She kept a watchful eye on me all day. Instead of our usual giggles, our walk home was somber.

While I was at school, Dad went to the police station to discuss his son's disappearance. Together with a couple of officers and a neighbor, they searched for Richard in Dad's wood patternmaking shop. Formerly an old lumberyard, the front portion contained his workbenches, tools and machines. Richard and he had been fashioning a walnut bowl for Mom. The lumber storage area was a dark, cavernous room that stretched all the way to the back alley. The men found no sign of Richard.

The police interviewed coworkers and other shop owners. They described Dad as being a good father and praised Richard as a well-behaved youth. They didn't believe Richard had run away, citing how much both he and Dad enjoyed their time together. They described how Dad taught Richard to use the tools and that he was talented, much like his father.

The police questioned neighbors, who also told how Richard and Dad were on good terms, spending much time together on hobbies of mutual interest. They disclosed that Dad would ground Richard if needed, but none of Dad's discipline was out of the ordinary. Others agreed that my parents were strict, but reasonable. One neighbor told the police that my parents "would do anything for you, if needed."

On the evening of January 19th, I crowded in behind a television news reporter and his camera technician who had set up in our living room. My parents sat together on the sofa with Dad's arm around Mom's waist. My eyes never left my parents' faces as they pleaded that anyone with information concerning my brother to contact the Pekin Police. Mom looked old with her face pinched. Dad had dark circles under his eyes and his lips were tight. Mom repeated that Richard experienced blackouts last October and she was concerned this illness may have returned.

After the media crew left, the phone rang. I was hopeful it was someone with news about Richard's return. Instead, Dad's eyes narrowed as he listened. When he hung up, he said it was a prank call. Dad contacted the phone company asking they put a trace on the call.

Afterward, Dad seemed restless. Pacing, his jaw clinched, he grabbed his coat and told Mom he was going for a walk. I had never known him to walk alone.

"Can I go?"

"No!" he snapped at me. "I need to be alone."

I stood in place as the door slammed. Immediately, my tears fell. Everything was so confusing.

That evening's newspaper reported the Pekin Police were cooperating with other agencies, seeking any clue or reason to explain Richard's disappearance. When asked if Richard met with foul play—a term I didn't understand—Police Chief Harris answered, "We are ruling out nothing." As I continued to read, I also learned that the twenty-four hour searches had stopped at dark the previous evening. I understood the logic behind the police's decision—that hundreds of searchers had not yet yielded a clue. There was no longer a need to send them out into the bitter air. My mind conceded, but my heart screamed, "No!" [1, 2, 3]

Deeply aware of the cold and loneliness of the night, I wanted to run out of the house into the dark, looking for Richard on my own. Instead, I just sat and stared at the carpet unable to think, to cry, or to help in any way.

The next day, my grandmother arrived to help with my care so I would not get behind on schoolwork. Dad and Mom spent their days searching: I yearned to do the same. I *needed* to be helping. I *needed* to be reassured that life was safe.

An assurance they could no longer make.

Grandmother was a highly intelligent, bookish woman. She had been widowed when I was very young, but meticulously grew three acres of roses and flowers while working fulltime as an industrial statistician for a large electric company. She cooked well and was kind, yet she seemed distant in this a stressful situation. I needed to be held and comforted.

What was worse, she was staying in Richard's bedroom. On the previous days, I often slipped into his room and touched his favorite things: his models, his Hot Wheels, and his books. I pressed my nose into his bed coverlet absorbing the scent of him. Now Grandmother had her clothes spread out on his bed. It was no longer a quiet refuge for me.

In the days following Richard's disappearance, neighbors, police, or reporters were often in the house when I arrived home from school. The police had traced the earlier call to Peoria, but no other information had been gathered. Lost in this new world of chaos in our house, I watched, invisible to the adults. Everything I knew had been turned inside out. I had no one to turn to. Normally both my parents took time to listen to both Richard and me and to offer affection. During supper, Dad had always asked about our schoolwork and made us laugh with his latest riddle or pun. Mom had always listened to us read and then led us in evening prayers. All that was gone.

Not only was my brother missing from my family, but hugs and laughter were as well.

The local newspaper paper contained a mixture of contrary thoughts and opinions. In one paper, my father publically thanked all the people who volunteered to search and the businesses that supported them.

> "We [my wife and I] were amazed at the number of people who took time off from work to help. People who don't even know us, [sic]. There were probably thousands of dollars spent in lost time and use of equipment, and for this we feel we owe all of you a deep debt of gratitude." [4]

In another newspaper, my parents expressed their concern that

Richard had been abducted or met with foul play. Both Dad and Mom were adamant: Richard was *not* a runaway. He was very intelligent. He would have made a plan; instead, all his belongings and money were still at home. Mom pointed out how he was eager to use his new toy train engine, adding he was too much a "tightwad" to have spent money on a new engine on Friday if he was planning to run away on Monday. [5]

Dad expressed his firm opinion that Richard had been abducted since the vast number of searchers had not yielded so much as a glove. Additionally, the police were admitting they had no clues or leads to follow. After all the extensive searches and interviews, nothing was discovered. [6, 7]

As for me? I finally understood the term *foul play*.

Unanswered questions zipped through my brain. What was happening? Why? Why would someone harm my brother? He was a kind and generous person. How do we find him? Will he come back to us alive? Where was God in all this? What's to keep me safe? From whom?

One evening, I wandered into my parents' bedroom as Mom was combing her hair. I walked up to her and wrapped my arms around her slim frame. She smiled at me as she untangled my arms. She invited me to sit beside her on the bed, then looked into my eyes and asked what was wrong.

"Everything." I sniffed. "Did someone harm Richard? Why, Mom? Why would someone do that? Why Richard? He would never hurt anybody. I miss him! And where is God? I thought He promised to help us. I don't understand anything."

Mom pulled me close, kissing the top of my head. "Sweetie, I don't have the answers. But trust God. That's all I have."

We cried together, holding onto one another.

That night, I crawled into bed discomforted. "Jesus, please be with my brother. Keep him safe and warm. Bring him home to us. Tell him I miss him." I wiped my tears and tried to sleep. Quiet was no longer my companion.

* * *

On January 21st, four days after Richard's disappearance, a local radio station, WSIV, offered a $500 reward for factual tips leading to Richard's whereabouts. Local citizens donated an additional $500, and later the Carpenters' Union, of which my dad was a member, another $500. These acts of kindness were a balm in the midst of turbulence.

Yet it was surreal to hear the reports about my own brother on the radio. In my mind, it was as if there was an invisible wall delineating life with Richard versus this current turmoil. One side was happy and safe; the other was sad, frightening, and confusing. I couldn't comprehend what was happening as well as what was not happening…

Richard was *not* walking in the backdoor, shouting, "I'm home!"

* * *

Much hearsay and many random tips came into the police. A pair of polyester jeans was found and brought to my mother for identification. Richard was wearing 100 % cotton denim blue jeans. Another pair of jeans covered with mud and some unknown substance was found, but laundered prior to being put in for evidence.

Seven sleds similar to Richard's and various other articles of clothing were discovered, but each was eventually discounted. Random possible sightings from as far as Colorado were checked. A young student reported to police that she had been feeding Richard in a barn outside of town. She later recanted. With each report our hopes flared only to be dashed when all the facts were presented.

On January 31, Dad telegraphed United States Attorney General John N. Mitchell requesting help from the Federal Bureau of Investigation (FBI). Dad desperately sought help from people more highly trained than the Pekin Police, who did not have one trained detective on staff at the time.

Dad also developed and organized a letter writing campaign to our elected officials at the federal level. He wrote the original draft and a friend typed a form letter any citizen could send to politicians:

> As a concerned friend of the Merle Griener family we are requesting the FBI's assistance in the search of their missing son.
> The Griener boy, Richard, age 13, never returned home from sled riding on January 17th.
> The Pekin Police Department had been unable to come up with a single clue altho [sic] in all fairness to them, they have expended many man-hours and have checked every lead.
> The parents of Richard Griener feel very strongly the boy hasn't run away and would appreciate any assistance the FBI could give our local police department.
> Sincerely,

Friends, neighbors and co-workers from the Carpenter's Union mailed these letters to the United States Attorney General John Mitchell, United States Senator Adlai Stevenson III, and United States House of Representative Robert "Bob" Michel. These letters pressured the FBI to respond publically. Don T. Sullivan, assistant agent in charge of the Springfield, Illinois, regional office, offered the use of their technical and scientific facilities to aid in the investigation. He publically acknowledged that the FBI was aware of the case; in contact with local authorities; and had created a missing person file on Richard. Nevertheless, Sullivan stressed, there was nothing to indicate Richard had been taken for ransom or carried across the state line, the two criteria for the FBI to step into the investigation.

After two weeks of daily searches, Dad reluctantly went back to work. He called home every day at noon to get an update to the investigation. Mom never had any substantiated nor hopeful information to share with him. After work, he searched. My dad came home late each night looking worn, with dark circles under his eyes. He was losing weight.

My closest friend carried me at school, reminding me of tests and upcoming assignments. I couldn't focus well. She offered both her compassion as well as her frustration that she couldn't help in any other way. What adult knew how to solve this problem, let alone two 11-year-olds? She couldn't make it right. No one could. At the end of our walk home, she looked deep into my eyes, cocked her head to one side, and sadly smiled at me. Then she squeezed my hand before I walked the rest of the way home alone.

I missed my brother so deeply it seemed beyond comprehension. I still fled to my closet to shut out the pain. I felt guilty for going about my day—being with Mom and Dad, staying in a warm house, and eating nice meals. The first joke I laughed at returned to slap me with shame for enjoying a moment. I lay awake often, thinking, wondering, and listening. Some nights, I opened my window in case Richard was close and calling to us.

Simple tasks were now painful. One evening, as I was setting the table, I burst into tears. "Mom, I don't know whether or not to put out a plate for Richard. What if he comes home while we are eating? Shouldn't there be a plate for him?"

We hugged each other tight as the tears flowed. We decided we would no longer set him a plate, but the empty spot at the table seemed to mock our attempts to continue on with life.

* * *

On February 2, 1972, there was a strange car in the driveway when I returned home after school. I raced into the house, my heart eager with curiosity. My mom, my grandmother, and two men in suits were engaged in a serious discussion. I could tell by Mom's expression that something was terribly wrong! Grandmother was pale. After Mom introduced one man from the Pekin Police and the other from the FBI, she went on to explain Grandmother had received a ransom call.

A ransom call! *That's good, right? Now there is the evidence of a crime and the FBI can help! A ransom call means Richard is alive!* My heart soared! They would help! They would find my brother! These men now had some clue to find him!

But Mom's tight expression told me that the news wasn't good. As Mom knotted a tissue in her hand, I heard them telling her things that didn't make sense. After a little while the somber-faced men left, but not before installing a portable tape recorder onto our phone to record calls. I could feel Mom's rigid muscles as she pulled me into her arms. Something else odd caught my eye. I turned to see Grandmother shaking and crying. I had never seen my grandmother cry.

"I'm sorry, Helen." Grandmother shook. "When I heard the man on the phone say, *money in a can,* I just became so frightened! I couldn't think straight. Everything became fuzzy. I couldn't even find a pencil to write it down. I am so sorry." She wrapped herself in a hug and hung her head. She removed her glasses to swipe at her eyes as Mom left my side to embrace her own mother. Then Grandmother quietly padded into my brother's room and shut the door.

Mom sat on a kitchen chair, wrapped her arms around my waist as I leaned against her legs. "Grandmother received a call this afternoon from a man. He said he had Richard and demanded money. Grandmother had become too shocked to remember any details. She missed any relevant directions that the caller spoke." I stiffened and turned to look at Mom's eyes.

Mom continued. "When the FBI and police arrived, we hoped she would be able to remember helpful clues, but she couldn't. She feels terrible about it. She feels she let all of us down, especially Richard."

"The FBI can find him now? Right?" Hope soared.

"They told us they had traced the call back to Peoria. But they don't believe there is any proof a federal law had been violated. They hold to the position that current laws block them from investigating further. As far as the police are concerned, the event is over."

We remained embraced, staring out the window, not speaking. I was trying to comprehend what I had been told.

After a bit, Mom went to lie down. I, though, was seething. Stunned, I sat on the sofa fuming. Questions pounded in my soul like storm waves against coastal rocks. Did the authorities think we were lying? Did we need a sign written in Richard's blood? What would spur them to take us seriously? Were they not advocates for Richard? For us? How much more did we need to endure? At what point did the police believe the family of a missing child? I wanted to throw rocks!

Anger led to judgments. Hard feelings formed against the police. I felt betrayed by them. Instead of serving and protecting us, my childish thoughts concluded, they were dismissing us as if we were a bother to them. *How do they know no federal law has been violated unless they investigate it further?* My little heart screamed! It seemed to me that the authorities were putting the burden of finding evidence on *us*. *Why* weren't they investigating the ransom call further? Craziness!

When Dad came home from work, my grandmother and mom came out of their rooms. The adults went into the kitchen to talk and I followed to listen. Dad stood rigid and hard as Mom explained what had happened. He reached for her hand, tears flowing from his eyes. Then he squeezed Grandmother's shoulder, assuring her that he understood her pain. Everyone was crying. I felt we had had been so close to some answers! Next, Dad turned to me and pulled me into an embrace. He held me tight as we cried together. Hope now lay shattered, like a fragile porcelain vase.

Mom laid out cold cuts for sandwiches, but no one ate.

Later I sat beside Grandmother and wrapped my arms around her waist. We nestled our heads together wordless, just holding on to one another.

That same day, Chief Harris told the press:

> "It's been nearly three weeks since the Griener boy vanished and it is very mysterious. The mysterious part of the whole situation is that with all the efforts that were made by so many people, there is not a single indication of what happened to the boy.
>
> "It's mysterious because other communities that have had cases of disappearances have had some clue to indicate what happened —whether he ran away, had an accident or met with foul play. But there isn't a single clue here and that is the big mystery to me." [8]

Five days later, a *Journal Star* reporter, Richard Kaston, wrote that neighbors saw Richard walking with the roll-up sled under his arm. Police verified the last known sighting of Richard was two blocks from home. [9]

By mid-February, the case was as cold as the winter air. The police hadn't generated any substantiated leads. Lieutenant Dale Riviere of the Pekin Police told reporters:

> "'The only thing we can verify is that he [Richard] was last seen by friends on the block of his home. We haven't eliminated anything.
>
> "'I hate to say it, but it's just like the kid was never alive at all,' he continued. 'It's almost like someone used an eraser on him.'" [10]

One day in late spring, before I left for school, Mom told me that some more volunteer searchers were going to use helicopters now that the snow had melted. Oh! How my heart ached to be with those pilots. Maybe Richard was still alive! I imagined the joy of squeezing my brother again! But I knew...

The volunteers were searching for Richard's body.

And as much as I hated to think it, even that would be better than the not knowing.

Later that morning at school, we heard the *wumpf! wumpf!* of the rotors as the search helicopter flew close to the ground over my school. All the students jumped from their seats to catch a glimpse of the helicopter. I, too, ran to the window. Unlike the happy children chattering about grand dreams of flight and adventure, I hoped I could see the pilots' eyes. Maybe even see what they saw.

I squeezed my eyes shut.

Something in my heart shattered at the sight of that search helicopter. Like the rotors chopping the cold air, grief chopped my heart. The weight of Richard's disappearance and possible death, added to the chaos of not having any answers, broke me. Overcome, I began to shake and gasp for air.

I turned away to see my gentle substitute teacher. I raced to her side, pressing my face against her huge pregnant belly. I just sobbed and sobbed against her dress. She held me, offering me a safe place to release my sadness.

Then she bent down, cupped my face in her hands, and asked, "Are you okay?"

I shakily nodded. She whispered for me to go to restroom to collect myself while she allowed the other children to continue giggling and dreaming their high ideas.

* * *

It seemed my caring and loving dad sought answers in a new way: He started drinking beer nonstop. He had always drank beer on weekends, but that soon became a habit in the evenings as well. He still worked during the week and puttered around doing home maintenance, but it was always with a beer can nearby. He was touchy and angry most days. I sidled up to him while he did his tasks, hopeful my help would cheer him.

My mom changed as well. She started looking wan and frail. She was always sad. She often lay down after work. Some days I sat on the bed next to her. She kept a handwritten Scripture on her bedroom mirror. Her faith seemed strong when she was weak. Curious, I asked her about the Scripture. We held hands and together read, "When the righteous cry for help, the LORD hears, and delivers them out of all their troubles. The LORD is near to the brokenhearted, and saves the crushed in spirit," (Psalm 34:17-18, RSV).

While I didn't understand all the words, when my mom looked at me I understood *brokenhearted*. I yearned to see her happy again. I *wanted* to trust Jesus to make it right.

"Mom, why did this happen to Richard? Why didn't God stop it?"

"I can't explain that. Some times bad things happen. But know, Jeanne, that God didn't do this. He loves us."

The situation didn't *feel* like God was loving. My faith was crumbling. I wanted to believe like Mom. She always had faith in Jesus. I wanted that. But it was like grasping snowflakes of faith and hoping they lasted forever.

* * *

One Sunday evening in early April, as we prepared for dinner, the phone rang. Mom answered and her face contorted as she listened. Dad's eyes grew wide, then his back became ramrod straight. He reached for the phone to take it from Mom, but she held up her hand.

Mom hung up and fell into Dad's arms. She buried her face in his chest. Dad embraced her, but I could see rage in his eyes. Mom mumbled something about a child's voice.

"Helen, I don't understand you. What are you saying?"

"It was a child's voice. Merle. He said he was Richard and he was being held for ransom. Oh, Merle!" She sobbed. "I don't think it was it was him, but what if it was?" She burst into tears again. I went to her side, trying to comfort her, but a spigot of questions and fears had just been opened in my own heart.

Dad called the phone company to put a trace on the call. Then he called the police. His eyes were fiery.

When the police arrived, Mom reported the child's voice didn't sound like her son.

Another meal forgotten....

I lay awake that night. Was Richard being held for ransom? Why? How would we get him back? What was happening to us? Why us? Was it legitimate? Who would tear at my mom's heart like that? Who would torment my parents that way? I understood the fire in my Dad's eyes as a burning desire to bring his son home, to protect us, and to see wrongs righted.

The next day, a Pekin Police captain followed up with the phone company, but they didn't return his calls until the following morning, two days after the original call. A trace required that a specially trained employee come to the main office to do the trace, and that hadn't happened.

The telephone company was no longer making tracing calls for us a priority.

Later, a juvenile was charged with making the prank call. My parents made a trip to the police station to confront the youth. No charges were filed and the youth apologized to my parents, but there was a hard edge about them when they came home.

* * *

In late spring of 1972, I still wasn't sleeping. Despite their own struggles, my parents noticed my deep sadness and thought having a pet would help. I had always loved animals, but Richard suffered from severe allergies. I promised I would give a puppy away the very minute Richard came home.

My dad came home a few days later with a beagle puppy. Such soft ears and tender eyes! However, we noticed some odd spots on her fur. A veterinarian told us the pup had five out of six intestinal parasites, as well as fleas and mange, but all were treatable. We nursed her to health and delighted in her silliness.

Once the pup was healthy, I snuck her onto my bed where I snuggled her as I fell fast asleep. This was a new version of puppy love.

One Saturday afternoon, I was running circles in the backyard with the pup jumping at me when my best friend came over. When I tripped and fell, the pup jumped on my chest and licked my chin. I bubbled with laughter. My friend watched. "It's good to see you smile again, Jeanne."

* * *

The spring and summer months brought no change in the case. Mom contacted a private investigator in New York who suspected foul play, but regrettably couldn't help. My parents didn't know of any other private investigators. They received letter after letter from psychics who simply stated what reporters had already described in detail. During this time, one of Richard's former doctors confirmed to police that prior to his disappearance he had completely recovered from a serious case of encephalitis. This had been the cause of my brother's earlier blackout and the foundation of Mom's fears that he had fallen ill on the sledding hill. But the doctor assured both my parents and the police that Richard had fully recovered.

By summer, the neighborhood was full of children running through sprinklers, climbing trees, and riding bicycles. Usually, our mothers gathered at the end of a driveway, iced tea in hand, chatting and laughing. Mom didn't smile much and walked away from the others quickly. When she stopped coming outside to gather with the other mothers I asked her about it.

"It's too sad to hear what their children are doing. It causes me to wonder what Richard would be doing if he was here. It makes me dwell on his absence. Hearing the other moms makes me sad.

I don't want to be rude, so I just go back to the house."

I hugged her. I wanted to make the sadness go away. I didn't know how.

Dad continued writing to elected officials pleading for the FBI's assistance in the search for his beloved son. When that didn't garner results, Dad suggested laws concerning missing children be changed. Vice President Spiro T. Agnew commended Dad's efforts on behalf of other families of missing children and spoke to FBI Director Hoover, Attorney General Mitchell, and our congressional representatives on Dad's behalf. But Dad had contacted those officials already back in January—to no avail.

In August, as other dads were planning family getaways, my dad was calling an Atlanta homicide detective, asking about a mass-torture-and-murder investigation of youths Dad had read about in a newspaper. He was hopeful the case would bring about a discovery of Richard's remains. Never mind how Richard could have arrived in Atlanta. That question and others could be answered after a positive identification of Richard's corpse was made.

Dad also contacted Chief Harris of the Pekin Police requesting they follow through with Richard's information. They did. Richard was not among the murder victims in Atlanta.

* * *

From May to December 1972, a specialized investigative team reviewed Richard's case. The Tri-County Intelligence Unit convened to offer advice, to follow up on leads the Pekin Police may have overlooked, and to find clues to Richard's case. They noted the lack of any one lead officer, the fact that no one was officially trained as a detective at the time of Richard's disappearance, the lack of accurate notes, and the inconsistent follow-up on information in the case. They investigated many suspects who had sexually assaulted young boys. The investigative team also traced my parents' phone calls, but those didn't reveal any wrongdoing. For all the work and effort, no new leads, no fresh clues were generated.

The entire year was an endless nightmare. Christmas was somber and bittersweet. Gentle reminders of Richard filled us as we hung his handmade ornaments on the tree. Sadness filled me as I finally lit the red Advent candle. Fear, anxiety, and anger marked the New Year, which began as the old year ended: without any answer to what had happened to my brother.

Would we ever know? Would we ever live in peace again? Where was the quiet I so valued?

5

Normalcy

1973-1979

So do not be afraid of them. There is nothing concealed that will not be disclosed, or hidden that will not be made known.
—Matthew 10:26 (NIV)

One year had passed and we were no closer to having answers than we were the first night of Richard's disappearance. My family established a rhythm, but the beat of life was off. In addition to tracing phone calls, pleading with politicians, disproving gossip, and giving media interviews, we added scanning crowds, reading personal letters from crazed madmen, getting fingerprinted, following investigations of mass murderers or predatory pedophiles, and challenging police inexperience. The new normal created constant vigilance for a clue to Richard's whereabouts or remains.

Mom paid the bills, bought groceries, and had gas put in the car. After the first year, when she again donned her RN uniform, it was as an obstetrics nurse, meeting the needs of new mothers and infants. She enjoyed rocking newborns to sleep, comforting them and making them feel safe. On her days off, she sewed clothing for us and gardened. Cooking, however, wasn't her forte'. Dad and I teased her a meal wasn't complete if it didn't include burnt peas. (Today I walk in her shoes: I enjoy gardening and sewing, but I am a court jester in the kitchen).

Dad had gone back to work after two weeks off, yet he didn't go back to his own shop for close to a year. He shared with us that he was flooded with painful remembrances of Richard when he stepped across the threshold. He completed a few contracts and then sold all his equipment.

Dad was skilled with his hands and liked to create, so he tried his hand at oil painting. Most evenings after my homework was completed, I joined him. He smiled and laughed as I squirmed my way onto his spinning stool next to his cluttered workbench in the basement.

One night I lifted a blank canvas to reveal an unfinished portrait of his son that Dad had started prior to Richard's disappearance.

"Dad, why didn't you finish this?"

"I don't know. I had planned to paint your portrait, too, you know."

"Why didn't you? You still can." I gave him an exaggerated smile.

"Yeah, I guess I can." His voice wavered. I looked up to see him wipe at tears. "I thought I would paint you both. I started with Richard because he was older. Both portraits were going to hang in the living room. I just can't seem to find the where-with-all to complete painting Richard's face. And it would be too painful to have just one on the wall." He messed my hair.

"I understand, Dad. It's okay." Then I squeezed him hard and long. The ache to be a whole family again remained unfulfilled.

* * *

On weekends, my family spent Saturday mornings doing chores. Mom always encouraged me with some extra spending money if I helped her weed the flower gardens. In the afternoons, I spent time at a friend's or watched sports on the television with Dad. In the evenings we enjoyed playing cards or board games. On Sundays, after Mom and I arrived home from church, we spread out in the living room reading the Sunday paper. During the week, while my parents worked, I went to school. When I came home I played with my dog, running circles with her in the backyard. The routine of life went on. These activities were the peaceful side of my life.

Yet there was a grueling and destructive side to my life as well.

* * *

On February 2, 1973, as we were clearing away supper dishes, the phone rang. Mom pressed the tape recorder and then answered the call. She mouthed that it was another ransom call. I froze. But Mom had the presence of mind to ask to speak to her son. Indomitable hope and fear warred within my chest. In the meantime, Dad ran into another room to use a different phone line to notify the telephone company to run a trace on the call. Mom stopped the recorder, and then hung up the wall phone, keeping her hand on the receiver. She rested her forehead against it and closed her eyes.

Dad came back in the kitchen, muttering. "The blasted telephone company doesn't have anyone working this evening who is trained to place a trace. They will have call in someone." Tipsy, he sing-songed the last words, swaying his head as his lips pursed.

Mom then released both her breath and her hand. I remained glued to the far wall. What will happen? *Is this a real clue?* Did someone still have Richard? Will the police help this time? My heart pounded against my chest and I felt light-headed. How can my parents even think?

Dad called the FBI. Perhaps this time, they would consider the tape recording the proof of wrongdoing that they needed to intervene. Perhaps. I could only hear one side of the conversation, as Dad answered very basic questions about Richard. His face became redder and his eyes narrower with each answer.

While not moving from my stance against the wall, I wanted to yank the phone from my Dad's hand. I screamed inside my head, *Mom, help!* We had another ransom call! Dad was talking to the FBI! But I could tell by hearing his side of the conversation that it wasn't going well. My heart pleaded, *"Please, be kind. The agent is just gathering facts. Please, don't make him angry. Please, don't let this clue slip away from us like all the others.* Please!"

I was sliding into a pit with no one to help.

The police came and recorded the event as a prank call. When the police seemed to disregard the situation, my mind raced and my heart skipped beats. Again, I felt betrayed by the authorities. It was all so confusing and hopeless.

After spending an agitated evening trying to complete my homework, I snuggled with my dog and cried myself to sleep.

After that incident, my sixth-grade teacher assigned me a novel set in the 1800s to help me "snap out" of my sadness. The main character in the novel lost a brother to influenza; yet, she learned to embrace life and to persevere. The teacher assumed several things. One, that I believed Richard to be deceased. I still clung to hope that somehow Richard was alive—I mean we had just had a ransom call a few days ago! At the same time, I presumed that he was dead. After one year without evidence, the oil of hope had never quite mixed with the water of reality.

The other assumption was that my family had closure—an enigmatic and elusive experience we had not yet attained.

Far from inspired, I was weighed down by the story. Was *anyone* ever happy?

Each night, at my desk, I tried to read the book. The more I read, the heavier I felt. So I decided: I would fail this assignment. Something I had never done before. (Or since).

The next day in class, I asked what the repercussions would be if I didn't turn in this project. As I had suspected, I had enough high marks to carry this one failed assignment. I stopped reading the book and didn't complete my assigned summation.

Nonetheless, the teacher didn't relent. On the day the book reports were due, after she gave all the other children new books to read, she called me up to her desk.

"Jeanne, what is this?" She held my unfinished book report.

"It's my book report. That's all I can do. I'll still pass. You told me that yourself."

"That's not the point." She raised her eyebrows at me. "I assigned this novel to you to learn about life. All the other students completed their assigned books and now have new selections. You, however, will not be allowed to go on until you complete *this* book report." She jabbed a sharp fingernail on my paper. "Finish the assignment."

We glared at each other. Flushed, I took my paper and slunk back to my desk.

I did push the boulder-novel uphill to comply with the teacher's demand. When I turned in my report, the teacher criticized my negative thoughts on the book, expounding that happiness could be found after tragedy.

Her advice was unwelcome at the time.

* * *

In 1973, my family wallowed with the unresolved reality of my brother's disappearance. At that same time, the United States of America was struggling with the formidable issue of our brave Vietnam veterans who were missing in action (MIA) or prisoners of war (POW). Several of my schoolmates began wearing copper bracelets with a service member's name and the date recording the capture or disappearance of that person.

It was a compassionate idea, to keep that veteran's name in the forefront of another who would then pray and think on the endangered military personnel. As I saw more and more POW/MIA-memory bracelets, I became aware that an overwhelming number of people felt as I, fighting the unknown fate of their loved ones.

One afternoon I told Mom about the copper bracelets. "Can I make one for Richard? He's missing and I could touch it as a reminder of him."

She motioned for me to sit beside her. "No, I don't think that is appropriate. These men died or went missing in service of our nation. I think a bracelet for Richard would dishonor those servicemen and their families."

"Missing is missing." My stomach tightened and I inched away from her. "It hurts the same."

"I know, sweetie. I know." She pulled me back into a hug, but I remained rigid. I tried, but failed to understand the deeper meaning. Emptiness nestled next to the desire to honor Richard in a tangible way.

That night I prayed. *God, how can I honor my brother?* In my mind, I saw myself as an A-student like Richard had been, and so I chose to become studious. No one else knew my decision, my vow to honor my brother this way. But it brought me special joy when I achieved high marks in school.

* * *

There were those, though, who dishonored us. Many times madmen mailed rants to our home. One individual wrote that my parents' faith in God was so weak that He punished them by taking Richard. Dad seethed, setting his jaw. Mom cried nonstop for days after receiving that rancorous letter. It sent me to my knees to pray that God would comfort my parents. My tenuous faith believed God was a loving, not punitive, Creator, like a lifeline to a drowning victim.

* * *

In spite of the trauma of losing one child, my parents strove to allow me to continue my activities and to grow in a healthy way. I was cognizant that they were trying to keep me safe even as they encouraged me to continue the ice-skating lessons that I had started years earlier.

However, the desire to be at the skating rink changed for me one day when police and sheriffs deputies gathered in the upper room of the ice arena. As I skated past, officers pointed their fingers in my direction. I was a grasshopper watched by a cat. I had no evidence of it, but I speculated they were discussing Richard's case.

The ice skating fun was squashed.

After supper that evening, I explained the situation—backwards. I started with, "I don't want to skate anymore." Before I could tell my parents how uncomfortable I had been that afternoon with reminders of Richard's investigation, or even utter another word, Dad, in a drunken state, slammed his fist on the table.

"You are nothing but a failure! You quit everything you start. You will never amount to anything."

How could he say such things? I looked at Mom, who offered a weak smile then looked at her plate. I jumped up. "That's not *true!* I want to stop because—"

Dad cut me off again, spouting more nonsense.

I fled the room. Curling into a ball with my dog, I nuzzled her face and wept. "That's not true!" I spoke aloud to the dog, to myself, and to God. I took a deep breath. Peace blanketed me. Stronger, I straightened my shoulders, lifted my head and declared, "That's not true!"

I did stop skating, but became active in other sports such as track and gymnastics. Both of my parents desired rewarding activities fill my days instead of the chaotic and often frightening events surrounding Richard's disappearance.

One summer day my best friend and I were bored, so we walked to the store to purchase cream pies. We were going to have a pie fight! Little did we realize the pies were not yet thawed. We laughed and laughed after I hit my friend with a rather hard banana cream pie. Silliness and giggles soothed our souls.

* * *

As I entered my freshman year in high school, the new people, the busier school, and the challenging academics excited me. A normal life could be found again! I had tucked the crime in it's own compartment in my brain and posted "Do Not Disturb" on the door. I made new friends and was making good grades in all classes except one. Geometry theorems eluded me. My geometry teacher was kind and funny, but still my grade in his class was almost failing. So I didn't think much about it when I was called out to see the guidance counselor. Here came the expected lecture on my poor grade in geometry.

Instead, the counselor asked probing questions about my

brother's disappearance.

I was whiplashed. Where did *this* come from? Why was he asking about this? Confused and uncomfortable, I tried to understand. Looking at him from the corner of my eyes, I kept my answers vague, not trusting his motives. Was this morbid curiosity? I squirmed under his intense gaze, eager to go back to class.

When he allowed me to return to geometry, I could not focus on what the teacher was saying. I stared at the clock, wishing the dismissal bell to ring. I'd been a carefree, goofy teenager when I came to school that day, but now was weighed in despair.

I didn't say anything to my mom. Surely it was a single odd occurrence. However, it happened week after week. Each time I met with the guidance counselor, I became nauseous and agitated, fighting the deep urge to flee.

I now believed Richard was dead, but no one could prove it. So I'd decided it was time to focus on going on with life. I didn't speak of the crime because there was nothing new to say. If an answer or new clue emerged, I would have been willing to share. Apart from that, I wanted privacy concerning the bizarre case surrounding my family.

I finally told my mom I didn't want to talk to this counselor any more about Richard's disappearance. I also requested we ask for a different guidance counselor. Mom agreed. I was so grateful for her support and protection. We celebrated with overflowing bowls of ice cream!

Later the first counselor apologized for upsetting me, explaining that he was trying to offer compassionate care. While I distrusted him for initiating the conversations, I respected him for ceasing when asked. And I slammed the anxiety his queries had created back into the "Do Not Disturb" closet of my brain.

* * *

Both my parents read newspapers seeking clues about Richard. They even had out-of-state relatives doing the same. Each news report of unresolved crimes against children could bring resolution to our own case. My parents followed cases nationwide of predatory pedophiles or mass murderers. They kept files on these perpetrators and we discussed them at the dinner table in the evenings.

How appetizing.

The police also delved into cases in other jurisdictions, interviewing perpetrators and discussing the case with medical examiners across the nation. The police were baffled. They reported to Dad and Mom that they had never experienced a case where an individual simply vanished. They, like us, were learning a new paradigm as we traversed such a puzzling and complex situation. Without clues, and without evidence, the case continued unsolved.

* * *

In 1975, after spending a summer afternoon swimming, I bobbed into the house. "Dad! I'm home!"

I found him in the basement, staring at Richard's workbench. "Dad, you okay?"

Without moving or looking at me, he said, "The police were here today. Seems they found an unidentified body in Ohio. They want us all to get fingerprinted."

I laughed. "That's a little late, isn't it?"

He shrugged his slumped shoulders. "It's better than never, I suppose." Then he turned to look at me. There was no light in his eyes. I couldn't think of anything to brighten his face. He wasn't the same dad of my childhood. In that tender father's place was a broken, angry man whom I deeply loved, but didn't know.

We embraced for a long time, neither speaking.

Using the family's fingerprints as elimination prints aided in identifying corpses. The request for *our* fingerprints was the result of one of the nationwide cases the police were following. The dental records they had already sent were inconclusive, so the Dayton, Ohio, coroner requested Richard's fingerprints. We found out later the child victim in Ohio had blue, not brown eyes, so even without fingerprints it obviously wasn't Richard.

* * *

Then, in the summer of 1976, perverse fate visited our town again. Another child was missing! My heart thudded and queasiness filled my gut as I read about Mark Helmig, nine-years-old, in the newspaper. I stared at the article, and then reread it, hoping to find a clue to his whereabouts. *God! Bring that little boy home alive unharmed. Don't let another family suffer the way we are. Help!* [1]

I took the newspaper into the kitchen where Mom was fixing supper.

"Mom, have you seen the paper? Another child is missing. It happened three days ago."

She whirled around and snatched the paper from my hand. She leaned hard on the edge of the table, so I eased her into a chair. Her eyes kept getting bigger and bigger as she read.

I finished supper preparations as she called a few friends, asking if they knew the family. It was the topic of conversation at the dinner table. Gruff and sharp, Dad challenged, "How can we let this happen? Why?"

"What can we do?" I asked.

"While these are good questions, we really don't have answers." Mom said. "I think I should go to the mother. I am the only one who truly knows how she feels. Perhaps I can offer her some advice or give her some comfort."

Dad grimaced. "It won't change the situation. Her son is missing. But if you feel it'll help, go ahead."

"Can I go, too, Mom?" Maybe I could help as well.

"I think it best I go alone, " she said.

No one had an appetite, as the meal sat cold.

* * *

The child's remains were discovered twenty-five days later in an abandoned rail boxcar. He had been stripped, bound, and murdered. When they found his body, I said a prayer of thanksgiving. Having a body was better than not knowing. Prior to the funeral my mother did visit his mother to comfort her. What a horrific basis to form a connection! [2,3]

That night, in bed, the world seemed unsafe again. At the least, Pekin was unsafe. With wobbly faith, I prayed. *God, why? Why a child? Do You see? Do You care? Why don't You stop it? Please, help the police find the culprit. Don't let him harm anyone else. I know You are Creator. I know You are Sovereign. But are You Good? Can I trust You?*

Now sixteen, I had started reading the Bible cover-to-cover. There had to be answers to those questions. Not understanding God's Zeal to have His chosen people live holy lives, I was repulsed by Old Testament stories of pillaging and annihilation. I yearned for a loving and active God. Yet, I kept reading. When I read Jesus' words and teachings, I finally started to comprehend the Father's Love for all people.

One day I came across a Scripture that gave my heart inexpressible Hope. It was Romans 8:28, "We know that in everything God works for good with those who love him, who are called according to his purpose," (RSV).

I sat beside my mother. "Look, Mom! God will use Richard's disappearance for our good. I have no idea how, but He says He will use all things for our good. That is the *only* way good can come out of this."

Usually faithful; instead, Mom shrugged as she flipped through a magazine. Undeterred, I held onto this promise like a lifeline.

For the first time in years happiness followed me as I had faith God would bring good of the tragedy. I was active in my youth group at church and did volunteer tutoring for special needs students in the summer months.

* * *

That newfound hope was tested in the summer of 1978, when the police again called my parents. Dad paled as he hung up the phone. "The police have made a 'promising' discovery. They have found a youth's decomposed body near railroad tracks in nearby Bloomington, Illinois." He swallowed hard. "The youth was found bound and had been murdered. They believe he had been sexually assaulted. This might be Richard."

Mom's hands flew to cover her mouth. "Oh, Merle." She jumped out of her chair to join Dad. They embraced.

My mouth twisted, then my stomach did the same. "What's next?" I asked.

Dad squeezed his eyes tight as he held Mom. "The police have Richard's dental records. They will compare those with the corpse. We'll know something in a few days."

The gruesome details of this child's last day haunted me. Sickened with the injustice and grieved by his suffering, I lay awake. Sleep eluded me.

Days later, Mom's face was pinched and pale as she told me the findings in Bloomington. I held my breath. I had yearned for so long for some answer to Richard's whereabouts, but her words delivered the final blow: it was another family's beloved child. Not Richard. Not ours.

Still no answers!

The remains were those of fourteen-year-old Marty Lancaster. He died in a similar manner to the Helmigs' child. A team of authorities from several jurisdictions was now working together for it appeared they had a serial killer preying on children in the area. [4,5]

At this time, Dad told reporters how hard it was to learn of children being assaulted and murdered. "'As far as I'm concerned there's no glimmer of hope. He's [Richard] dead, murdered. I've felt like that from the beginning, but it gets worse every time something like this happens.'" [6]

That evening, I raced outside to our swing set, which I still loved even as a teenager. I pumped air as hard as I could. My legs went higher and higher as my hopes went lower and lower. *Why, God? Where is justice? Why the suffering? Are You trustworthy? Where is the Good? Will we ever have answers?* My hopes flew away in the wind. The faith I had gleaned weakened by each act of violence.

* * *

Christmas 1978 was no different. Just after the holiday, Dad received yet another call from the police. He again relayed gruesome news. The police suspected Richard might have been a victim of John Wayne Gacy, Jr., a Chicago-area contractor. The police again sent Richard's dental files to the Cook County Coroner. [7]

After being under surveillance for a month, Gacy turned himself in to the Des Plaines, Illinois, police. He admitted to police to that he had sexually assaulted and then murdered males from twelve to twenty-nine years of age. He then buried their remains on his property or described how he tossed their bodies into the nearby river. Charged with the murders of thirty-three individuals, he became known as one of the worst mass murderers in United States' history to date. [8,9]

The Cook County, Illinois, Coroner put out a nationwide plea for families and police to help him identify all the bodies recovered. Gacy was known to pick up some of his victims from bus stops. At that time, Illinois had a law that, without a positive identification of the corpse, Gacy couldn't be charged with the homicide. [10]

I just stared at Dad. I could *not* do this again. After hanging out with friends, laughing and stuffing our faces with pizza, I had come home to learn that my brother might be among a deranged man's victims. One minute, life was peaceful and fun, then the next I was on high alert, anxious with horrific speculations darting through my head.

The grueling, crazy cycle of a two-sided normalcy kept spinning.

We had had plans to celebrate the New Year playing cards with neighbors. I didn't want to go. I wanted to stare at the wall. I wanted off this carnival ride of horrors, sorrows, and hopes deferred. My faith, now weak as a snowflake, had melted. Numb and weary, I reined in my heart—perhaps too much so: I felt no sorrow, no angst, and no compassion.

The New Year came in without me. Just days after New Year's Day 1979, the police reported to us that Richard was *not* among Gacy's victims.

I stuffed the renewed frustrations and sorrows into deep crevices of my mind, and the room with the *Do Not Disturb* sign expanded. The following months I distracted myself with finishing well in high school to then heading to college. I graduated high school with honors, having kept my vow to honor Richard with high marks. Just days before I was to leave for college in the summer of 1979, the police revealed a suspect in the deaths of Mark Helmig and Marty Lancaster. This time, as I read the description of the suspect in the newspapers, my heart hammered louder with each word. The suspected perpetrator, William J. Guatney, was nicknamed Freight Train...

Because of his ability to imitate a freight train whistle. [11]

This fit the description of the odd man we had encountered at the hobby store just days before my precious brother went missing! The man I had called evil seven years prior, and the current suspect in the Helmig and Lancaster murders, had the same description! Could *he* have harmed my brother?

Dad was still at work as I picked up the evening paper and thrust it into Mom's face. "You must read this! I'll stir the food." She paled as she read the description. "This is like the man in the hobby store! Do you think he took Richard?"

Her conclusion unnerved me. "I do, Mom. He whistles like a freight train. How many people can do that?"

Guatney lived as a drifter, hopping train cars to travel across the Midwest. He often worked at summer carnivals and small town fairs. His friends said he would go crazy when he was drinking, describing him as mean and terribly strong. He described Helmig's and Lancaster's clothing and their demeanors in detail. Yet, he stopped short of admitting to killing the boys, and he was never charged with their murders. The local police departments could not find enough evidence against Guatney to press charges. [12]

The whirls of college life distracted me from following the case. I was confident my mother would speak to the police about our suspicions that Guatney and the man in the hobby store in 1972 were the same. One investigator believed Guatney was responsible for taking Richard, but his fellow detectives dismissed the idea because the man's other victims met their fate during the summer. They had no way to prove that the strange man in the hobby store two days prior to Richard's disappearance was, in fact, Guatney.

In time, Guatney was charged with the murders of several other boys in both Nebraska and Kansas. After many legal proceedings, he was found to be mentally incapable of standing trial due to organic psychosis from alcohol consumption. He was committed to a mental institution, where he remained until his death in 1997. [13]

(I do not know if the police ever spoke to Guatney about Richard. He certainly was never charged with my brother's death).

* * *

By now, I didn't believe justice for Richard would be served. I went off to college an angry young woman. I was angry because of the cruelty and violence in life. And now I was angry with God. I saw Him as fickle: a God who capriciously brought benevolence to some people's lives, while others were to suffer. I was angry because I had no idea how to move His Hand to my favor. He had not protected my brother! God had not brought him home, nor had He brought good out of the situation.

I was angry that my parents, too, had changed for the worst. Dad drank too much and Mom was depressed. But me...

I was *angry*.

Richard in the go-cart he had made with me pushing! Source: Helen Griener

Dad took this picture of Richard as his source for
a portrait he started to paint of his son.
Source: Merle Griener

Richard and me opening Christmas gifts, 1971.
Source: Merle Griener

Richard, Mom and me playing board games, Christmas 1971
Source: Merle Griener

MISSING
PEKIN, ILLINOIS

RICHARD WILLIAM GRIENER

White Male   13 yrs. old   Dark brown hair, brown eyes
5 ft. ht.   approx. 90 lbs.

MISSING SINCE JANUARY 17, 1972   5:30 PM

Last known to be wearing gold colored nylon jacket with hood attached, long brown ski mask, blue jeans, green insulated boots, carrying a blue plastic toboggan. Home: No. 8 Brentwood Ct. Pekin, Illinois.

Anyone having information concerning the above child please contact:
GEORGE V. HARRIS
CHIEF of POLICE
PEKIN, ILLINOIS

Missing Poster, Source: *Pekin Daily Times*, (Pekin, IL), January 16, 1973, pg. 19, col. 6-9.

1994, four generations enjoy life together—my son, Daniel; my father, Merle; my mother, Helen; my grandmother, Mabel, and myself. Source: Merle Griener

Dad and Mom celebrating their 50th wedding anniversary.
Source: Author

6

Yearning

1979-1986

Delight yourself also in the LORD, And He shall give you the desires of your heart.
—Psalm 37:4 (NKJV)

Over the next several years, I kept the "Do Not Disturb" sign firmly in place over the portions of my heart that held the horror, trauma, grief, and subsequent distrust of others. Yet, next to that room was a yearning for answers that pushed incessantly at the locked door. There was always an inner friction.

Disquiet within me continued through my college years as I trained to become a special education teacher. However, one educational theory offered a modicum of peace. The Schema Theory surmised that the brain was predisposed to bring closure. If one read *wrd*, he automatically knew that was *word*. The theory concluded that we humans were hardwired to draw conclusions from facts, perceptions, and experiences.

This was both a great revelation and a relief to me. I finally understood that constant gnawing at my soul to find my brother.

I now knew it was not abnormal to ever yearn, to ever wonder, and to ever hope for answers. That simple theory cracked the angry shell around my heart. The anger was replaced by profound questions. Did God create me with a need for closure? If so, why didn't He answer? Was He trustworthy? Was God Good? The questions were the beginning of tentative conversations with God.

While in college, Dad found work in northern Illinois. Dad and Mom sold the house in Pekin in 1980 and moved. (Prior to the move, the reward fund was refunded or redirected to a charity by the bank holding the account). While the places in Pekin could no longer haunt them daily, the drink followed Dad. In 1984, Mom insisted that Dad get treatment for alcoholism. Dad achieved his sobriety then and maintained it until his death at 89. My old dad came back—the one who was compassionate, funny, and wise. Mom also grew stronger and happier. I started to rebuild my relationship with both of them, enjoying their company on frequent weekend visits.

After graduation, I acted on the need for closure. I purchased a plot in a cemetery and had a headstone erected in Richard's name. The family now had a tangible way to honor Richard. After that, Dad, Mom, Grandmother, extended family members, and I made annual trips to the cemetery to lay flowers at his stone. We all knew that neither a body nor even a coffin lay under the soil, but it was enough to be able to lay a bouquet to show our love. It helped to ease the gnawing that had eaten away at so much of my heart. It seemed to help the others, too.

A few months later, though keenly aware of how alcohol had harmed my family, I willfully decided to get drunk to escape life's burdens. I didn't want to simply ease the pain; I wanted to escape. I spent one week as a working drunk—teaching elementary students by day, staying drunk every waking hour at home. I enjoyed the numbness the alcohol created. The only glitch was going to church hung-over. That hypocrisy and the awareness I was genetically predisposed to becoming an alcoholic myself jolted me sober! I never drank again.

Yet to what else could I turn to ease the pain of living, to quiet the unanswered questions? The emptiness, the unknown and the sadness were always present.

As I pondered the grief still in my heart, somehow, deep within my soul, the promise of God from Romans 8:28 sang out: He will bring Good of all things to those who love Him! I remembered that from nine years earlier, when I was sixteen. Hope glimmered, but immediately it was dimmed by a deeper question: Was God Good?

It was as if a part of me wanted to have hope in a Good and Loving God despite my skewed perception of Him as untrustworthy. God seemed dangerous to me, allowing a vulnerable thirteen-year-old boy to vanish!

For the next year I waffled between anger, distrust, and hopelessness and a deep yearning to believe in a loving and kind God.

Then one snowy day, late for some appointment, I sped on the highway, traveling up a blind curve. Suddenly my little car began spinning out of control. I couldn't navigate for the fury of the steering wheel's spin! I had to let go!

I spoke aloud. "God, if You are real, I could use some help right now."

Peace suddenly consumed me as my car spun crazy circles in the highway; then started sliding sideways. I looked to my left—my body was perfectly in line to crash into a utility pole. I knew the impact would seriously injure me or even kill me. But I had Peace.

The car stopped four inches from the pole!

Awed, I crawled across the seat to exit the car. Not even a scratch on the car or me! A real God had just saved my life and granted me peace. I was undone with wonder and thanksgiving.

God was real! God was close! God cared! I thanked Him, but one question still gnawed at me—one I didn't know how to articulate apart from appearing ungrateful. I hated that it was there, but knew, too, I couldn't advance without an answer to it: Was God Good? Could I depend on Him with my life?

After my supernatural near-miss, I read the Bible daily, watched a television evangelist, and sang to the Lord. I knew my heart was getting softer as I grew more desperate to find truthful answers. A couple of my close friends, who had themselves become Christians, ministered to me. They answered my questions about God, provoked my faith, and spoke in tongues of the Holy Spirit. I was contrite for my sins while grateful for their ministry to me.

Then, in early spring, I heard a tele-evangelist say she was going to speak a prayer to receive Jesus into one's heart. I knelt in front of the TV, placed one hand on the screen, the other on my heart, and repeated the prayer aloud, hoping Jesus was listening. Again, the Peace covered me. Suddenly I was full of Joy! I couldn't stop smiling!

Having been raised in a Christian home, I believed Jesus was God's Son come in the flesh. I believed He died for my sins and I believed God raised Him on the third day. Jesus was my Savior. But now, I accepted Him to be Lord of my life. My Savior and Lord. Gone were the heaped piles of rotten distrust. God knew and cared!

The next morning, I was singing to the Lord Jesus with an overflowing heart. Then I realized I was singing in a foreign tongue, unlike anything I had ever heard. Due to the Peace and Joy I was experiencing, I assumed it was the same tongue from the Holy

Spirit as I had witnessed in my friends. I was unafraid and continued. Oh, the hope that came into my heart! I felt so alive!

I tearfully prayed the words of Romans 8:28. "Lord Jesus, I don't fully understand how You brought Good of my brother's disappearance, but You have. For because of it, I have sought You out. I have found You and You have given me Your Salvation. I am saved because of Richard's disappearance. I have You as my Lord. That is some Good that has come out of it. I am confident You are loving and kind.

"However, I do not understand why he had to die or why You didn't stop it. Where were You? Did You care? Can You still be trusted? Are You truly Good? I want to know more. I have faith You will help me find those answers. Thank you, Jesus."

I was now ready to submit to His Leadership while I sought His Answers to the questions that had gnawed on my heart for so many years.

7

Forgiveness

1987-1995, 2019

> *[Jesus speaking] "For if you forgive other people when they sin against you, your heavenly Father will also forgive you. But if you do not forgive others their sins, your Father will not forgive your sins."*
> —Matthew 6:14-15 (NIV)

An awkward dance between Jesus and me ensued as I matured in faith. With tender compassion, He choreographed our dance so that I gained more confidence in Him with each step. Yet, my questions about His Trustworthiness and Goodness caused me to stumble. When I was feeling afraid, I tried to take back the lead. With each turn, Jesus restored my innate ability to perceive more than the natural elements. Throughout the dance, the Spirit of Truth, God's Spirit, sang songs of deliverance over us as we waltzed through life together. As I grew in faith, our dance became beautiful.

While I still had questions about Jesus's role in my brother's disappearance, I accepted He was Sovereign, so He was never obligated to answer my questions. Rest came by trusting Him, regardless of the earthly results. So I was unprepared for the next thing the Holy Spirit showed me.

One day, I was worshipping the Lord, singing in the Spirit, with my hands raised. Suddenly, in my mind's eye, I was at the railroad tracks in Pekin, with Jesus beside me. On the ground, near an open boxcar, my brother knelt with his hands tied behind his back. His feet were bound as well. He saw us and smiled. Then Guatney came into view. He roared and delivered a powerful kick to my brother's side. He began to crush Richard with his powerful legs and weight, stomping my brother's torso.

I was screaming at Jesus to *do* something!

Instantly, Jesus covered my brother with His Body, shielding Richard by a Holy Presence. The blows went through Jesus to my brother. I stared, mouth agape. Jesus's Presence allowed Richard courage and peace. My brother's face showed no terror or pain!

Was this perhaps similar to what the martyr Stephen had experienced? Jesus didn't stop the murderous assault on Stephen, but He gave him Peace in the process of dying. In this way, Jesus manifested the depths of His Love.

Jesus was *with* my brother through all the cruelty, madness, and pain. In my vision, my brother died peacefully in the midst of great evil. And I learned I could trust Jesus no matter what. Circumstances were not resolved as I hoped, but God was Sovereign. I now believed that He went with me through all things and that He truly brought Good from all I had endured, (Romans 8:28, paraphrased).

After my shock of the vision wore off, other questions pestered me: *Why, God? Why don't You simply stop the madness? Why allow the cruelty and violence?*

God again answered in a profound way. He directed me to His great love for *everyone*.

The mass murderer in Illinois, John Wayne Gacy, Jr., had briefly been a suspect in my brother's disappearance. In my harsh opinion, the man was a monster who deserved the death sentence the state of Illinois imposed on his life. The execution date was set for May 10, 1994.

I purposed to celebrate it.

That evening, with praise music blaring from the stereo, I sang and danced a celebratory dance. The hideous Gacy was going to die and the world would be a safer place. Around 12:20 AM, after I was sure the lethal injection had done its work, I paused to rest. Firmly and sadly, I heard in my spirit the Heavenly Father ask, "Are you done yet?"

"What do you mean? I thought You would be pleased with my dance."

The Heavenly Father answered, "Daughter, that man was My creation—he just didn't know it. My Son died for him."

I gasped! A new paradigm stilled my dancing feet: God loved John Wayne Gacy, Jr. God had wanted him forgiven, redeemed, and in Heaven with Him. I recalled the words in the Gospel of John 3:16-17, NKJV:

> "For God so loved the world that He gave His only begotten Son, that whoever believes in Him should not perish but have everlasting life. For God did not send His Son into the world to condemn the world, but that the world through Him might be saved."

Then, like a chalkboard in my brain I saw "...for all have sinned and fall short of the glory of God," (Romans 3:23, NKJV).

Christ died for me before I accepted Him because He knew I would sin—just like He died for Gacy, knowing Gacy would sin.

God loved us both. The depths of His Love for humankind overwhelmed me.

My head spun as the Holy Spirit further challenged, leading me to Matthew 5:21-22, NIV:

> [Jesus speaking] "You have heard that it was said to the people long ago, 'You shall not murder, and anyone who murders will be subject to judgment.' But I tell you that anyone who is angry with a brother or sister will be subject to judgment. Again, anyone who says to a brother or sister, 'Raca,' is answerable to the court. And anyone who says, 'You fool,' will be in danger of the fire of hell."

This was more than I could bear! God didn't look upon sin as I did. In front of God, I was no different than Gacy—sin is sin. While I couldn't call Gacy a brother or sister in the faith, this passage illustrated to me the sensitivity of the God's desire for us to live with pure motives. Instead, I harbored hatred in my heart for him, in essence, murdering him with my thoughts. I certainly had not wanted him alive and redeemed.

I sank to the floor and closed my eyes. *Father! Help! Forgive me!*

I was undone and humbled. I had to ask God to forgive me for harboring murderous thoughts concerning a man who had inflicted unconscionable harm on others. God didn't see him through hideous eyes like I did. And that meant something else.

I had to forgive Guatney with the same Grace.

Father! This is too hard for me!

In the book, *The Shack*, by Wm. B. Young, God described forgiveness as letting go of the perpetrator's neck. He was talking to a character named Mack, who had lost his vibrant daughter to a homicidal pedophile. Mack wanted to destroy the murderer. Such justifiable rage and anger! Yet God required Mack to forgive. When Mack couldn't do it, God gently explained that forgiveness was letting go of the perp's neck. What happened to the culprit after that was not Mack's responsibility. This was a most profound example of forgiveness. [1]

I needed Grace to let go of both Gacy's and Guatney's necks. I didn't have it within myself to do it, but I knew God was requiring it of me as Jesus offered His supernatural strength. I stayed in a place of prayer, telling Jesus how challenging this process was until the hatred, angst, and bitterness toward both mass murderers flowed out of me. Only with Jesus' Help could I have done that!

Now, proud of how shiny I thought my heart looked, I leapt! *Look at me, Jesus!* He smiled back, but then told me to sit on the bench for a bit. He had another step in mind.

The precious Holy Spirit revealed other less significant players in my brother's disappearance toward whom I harbored harsh and negative attitudes. Names and faces of those involved in the case flashed in my mind: my parents, teachers, neighbors, police officers, psychics, FBI agents, politicians, and yes, even, myself.

How could I *not* have recalled the events of the hobby store until years later?

God commanded me to forgive all.

It was difficult. I had to stop often, and sometimes I cried. Sometimes I even threw rocks. As Forrest Gump said, "Sometimes, I guess there just aren't enough rocks." [2]

Again, I needed the Grace of Jesus. Hatred and judgments were not mine to carry. I started by describing the offense, telling Jesus of the pain others' choices had caused me. Then I symbolically gathered up those infected wounds and gave them to Jesus, who had finished His work on the Cross. He then filled the painful areas with a sweet healing salve.

This process of forgiveness was done repeatedly as different aspects of the traumatic events unfurled in my thoughts. As others had fallen short of perfection, I had, too. So I blessed all involved with Truth and Peace in Christ Jesus.

Jesus had a special gift for me when it came to forgiving myself, though. I had a vision of being in a beautiful sea, with clear, cerulean waters. I was swimming in the depths, with no clear understanding of how to rise to the surface, yet no fear either. While I was swimming, I was acutely aware of my loneliness and unworthiness. Then suddenly a dolphin appeared. He nudged me, laughed, and nudged me again. He allowed me to hold onto his dorsal fin as he swirled, plunged to the depths, and then raced to the surface. His leaping and twirling had me laughing by the time we made our way to the beach.

The dolphin swam away as I walked onto the beach with Jesus there to greet me. I commented on how freeing that felt. He told me I had just been in the sea of forgiveness. He had received special permission to allow me to be there, yet He firmly told me I was never to swim there again.

He placed His Hand on my shoulder and smiled at me. "Jeanne, your sins are forgiven. You are washed clean with the water of My Word. Richard's disappearance was not *your* fault."

I was flooded with tears of relief. I stood crying for minutes as the vision faded, but the forgiveness and cleanliness remained tangible to my soul.

* * *

The forgiveness I had offered was tested by fire in 1987. On one of my weekly calls home, Mom shared that the Pekin Police were reviewing the case. Again. Mom told me that with the help of the same misguided psychic who had taken my brother's slippers the first day of his disappearance, the police were now pursuing *Dad* as the person of interest, despite employers, neighbors, and friends all affirming him. It was *not* Dad.

A close family friend had called my parents to tell them the police were busting up the basement and that the ground around the foundation of the old house was trenched. Back in the 1970s, while I was still living there, one basement wall had shifted due to soil heaving and compacting. The damage was bad enough that in one area we saw daylight through the basement wall. Dad often tried to tuck point the mortar to keep rainwater out. And what changes had occurred to the house in the seven years after my parents sold it?

That weekend I visited my parents to see how they were faring in the face of this horrific new development. During supper Dad didn't tell us a joke or share a political opinion. After supper, he pulled on a sweater and stared at his mug of hot tea.

Odd.

When he excused himself to the garage to piddle at his workbench, I followed. I squirmed onto his swivel stool like I had as a child. "What's wrong, Dad?"

"Nothing. Why do you ask?"

"I don't know," I said. "You seem sad."

He stopped sanding the block of wood in front of him. Eyes averted, he said, "I suppose I am." He looked old.

"Can I help?"

"No, sweetie. I don't think so."

"Dad," I said, "I know the Pekin Police dug up the basement and all around the foundation of the old house. I know they were looking for Richard's remains. And I know they suspect you of murdering him."

His shoulders drooped further as he turned to look at me. His eyes held such deep sorrow.

"But I also know you would never, *ever* harm Richard or any of us. Under that gruff exterior is a tender heart. Every fiber of my being knows you are innocent. You loved Richard. I know that. Mom knows that. Your friends know that. We believe in you. Besides, you turn green at the smallest drop of blood."

He smiled at my attempted joke and patted my knee.

"Thanks, sweetheart. That means a lot to me, " he said.

There was no evidence to justify such an exhaustive, expensive, and expansive search of our old house. It was destructive to both the house and my father. This became the fight of his life—a test of his ability to love well in spite of speculations perpetuated against him.

My heart thudded. How could I help him?

Prayer! That was the answer! My family was in a battle, so I prayed that God would strengthen and protect my parents. I prayed the Truth would rise to the top, like cream. I prayed the Peace of Christ would guard them. This prayer was answered as they agreed to talk to police yet again.

That Peace covered both my parents as they complied with more police interviews and polygraph tests. They answered questions, and then each passed the polygraph tests. No conclusions and no charges came from this painstaking investigation.

* * *

Dad and Mom also never stopped seeking answers. In 2009, they offered DNA samples to the National Center for Missing and Exploited Children. In 2016, I requested that the DNA samples be uploaded to a new national clearinghouse created by the

Department of Justice. This was available to all authorities and families dealing with missing persons. [3]

By 2019, I'd reached the point in my faith dance that I thought I was ready to go *en pointe*. Instead I tripped.

The day after the Illinois State's Attorney General (AG) was inaugurated in 2019, I received a call from a retired Pekin Police officer. He was cordial, stating he was doing investigative work for the local state's attorney. The AG was hoping to clear up some old cold cases, especially unidentified remains of Gacy's victims from 1978. Both this officer and the local state's attorney had participated in the destructive search of my childhood house and had pursued Dad as a person of interest in 1987. The former cop asked for my DNA sample to make comparisons. I told him I would consider it and ended the call. I couldn't believe it!

Heart pounding and jaw clenched, I stared hard at the trees outside. Why? Why was he calling me? Was this politically motivated? Why had he not searched for that information before disrupting my life? Why? Why? *Why?* Why had he *not* done his due diligence in locating my parent's DNA in the national database? Why be so insensitive to me? What may have been a simple request on his part flooded me with painful memories of the endless cycles of hope deferred and the lack of advocacy by the police.

Why?

I called him back and I reminded him where he could find the data he was seeking. As far as I know, the remains were not Richard's. [4]

Nevertheless, God used that to bring Good. My sharp, angry reaction revealed a tear in a tendon of my heart. No toe shoes yet! I needed to forgive yet again. *Again.* God's Love was so pure that He was concerned with all that I faced, leading me to love and dance well. His Desire was that I live free and unhindered by anger, judgments and unforgiveness. What a high standard He held before me! Yet, being a kind dance master, He never expected me to forgive alone. Jesus taught me by His own example the importance of forgiveness. As He hung dying with excruciating pain, He cried out to the Father to forgive us, (Luke 23:34, NIV, paraphrased). He required no less of me.

Jesus choreographed the steps and provided the music as I followed Him in yet another dance of forgiveness. This time, however, I wasted no time in following His Lead. I knew He required forgiveness for my own good, as well as the others involved. The required forgiveness was given, and my heart healed from its tear. I wanted Jesus more than anything! And I had learned the goodness that came from forgiving.

8

Mountains

1996-2021

He has shown you, O mortal, what is good. And what does the Lord require of you? To act justly and to love mercy and to walk humbly with your God.

—Micah 6:8 (NIV)

Besides the vitality of forgiveness, Jesus had other lessons for me. Lessons I needed to learn in order to be free of doubt and angst. The arduous process to learn these answers was not instantaneous. Over time, I gained comprehension by reading the Bible and asking the Holy Spirit to reveal Truth, helping me understand God's Heart. Jesus came to give me abundant Life. I was hungry for His Answers.

So, daily, in the quiet of my farmhouse, as the open window carried a gentle breeze filled with birdsong past the cotton curtains, the Holy Spirit led me to questions that created an imposing mountain range in my faith journey. Forgiveness was one thing, but what about Justice? Between them, mass-murderers Guatney and Gacy assaulted and killed over fifty youths. Was I to overlook that? Did God? Why was there evil? Who was to receive Mercy? And what did Godly Justice look like?

The questions gave me pause. I could ignore, even deny God, and find answers on my own. Or I could submit these new questions to Him as I had with my other questions, allowing Him to reveal His Answers in His Time. I continued to study the Bible, asking the Holy Spirit to reveal Truth concerning these weighty matters. I was confident God's Love and Wisdom would help me traverse these formidable, faith-crushing peaks.

The first mountain to climb was the foreboding and persistent question of why. *Why, as a Sovereign and Loving God, did you allow my brother to suffer? Why did You not stop it?* The sharp rocks of why hurt.

The answers were in the fact that God desired freethinking and therefore, free-loving creatures. I realized He created us all with a free will. The description of Adam in the book of Genesis revealed God's Desire that we would submit our free will to Him because He was worthy and loving. On the positive side, we humans could choose Jesus, choose life, and choose love. On the negative side, we could choose evil, death, and hatred. Sometimes a person chose his or her own twisted way to overpower another. God allowed our choices, so He didn't always stop others' malevolence. Instead, He brought Good out of terrible situations for those who love Him, to in turn, use us to bring comfort to others' sufferings.

All in all, God was immutable, all-knowing, all-seeing, ever-present, flawless, pure, and longsuffering. I imagined Him in Heaven, looking at billions of wayward children, some of whom were shaking their little fists in His Face. The fact that He didn't simply blow us all away and start afresh, removing our free will, creating automated yet loving creatures, was evidence that He believed in His Plan. As free-will creatures, we had the choice between Heaven or

Hell based on our relationship with Jesus, God's Son, who came in the flesh, lived, died to atone for our sins, and rose again.

Either we accepted Him as Savior and Lord or rejected Him. Believing in Jesus was the best choice I ever made! Yet, all in all, God dignified *each* of us with the freedom to choose.

The next mountain was this: Did God allow evil? Or did *we* allow evil by our free-will choices? God was loving, not the author or producer of evil. As I read about Jesus' Compassion as He healed and delivered *all*, I saw Him as Kind. He never scolded those hurting or broken. In contrast, the activities of the mass murderers that preyed upon the innocent confirmed that some people did choose evil. I believed that God created and then honored humanity's free will. Evil was ours—humankind's—to accept or reject.

When tragedy slammed into my life, I turned inward to protect and insulate myself from pain. Yet God did not want me to be the source of my own strength. He was exceedingly caring, ever-present, and empathetic. He certainly understood my pain. His Only Begotten Son was struck down violently, cruelly, and seemingly prematurely. I pondered this for some time and concluded that Jesus was *not* murdered.

I came to understand that murder involved a surprise attack. Murder involved being overwhelmed by another's rage or jealousy. Murder involved a victim. Murder involved one taking another's life against the victim's will. None of those descriptions fit Jesus' death on the Cross.

Yes, others killed Jesus, but His Death was unique. He knew the attack on Him was imminent; He knew the timing of the events to follow. He died as the result of others' rage and jealousy, yet it did not overwhelm Him or surprise Him because He had already agreed to the Father's plan. In fact, He did that before there was Time. He went *willingly* to the Cross out of His great love for humans. He *gave* His Life as atonement for our sins. He then overpowered evil when He descended into Hell and was resurrected. He gave Himself so that we might have eternal Life in Heaven, should we choose Him.

Jesus was *nobody's* victim.

So while God allowed free will in humankind, thereby, allowing evil to exist, He did something magnificent about its undesirable effects. He sent His own Son, Jesus, to become sin for each of us and to overpower it. Free will explained why there was evil, and the Cross explained why there was Hope.

Then came the mountain of whether or not God overlooked the evil in the world. Did He let the wicked go unpunished? I had to forgive mass murderers, but did that mean they got a free pass? What about those who had lied or gossiped or used divination against us? Did having free will allow them to skip through life unhindered?

Back when I danced at Gacy's execution, God told me He loved everyone, and that He sent His Son to die for each and wanted each soul redeemed and restored and resurrected in Heaven with Him. What was I to do with that? Could I live in Heaven with redeemed murderers and liars and psychics? Would I?

Full of myself, I wanted to climb down off this particular mountain and walk away.

However, I persevered, clawing up this gnarled mountain of whether or not the wicked went unpunished. God reminded me how I loved to be forgiven when I made selfish choices. Jesus taught in Matthew 5:7, NIV, "Blessed are the merciful, for they will be shown mercy." How I delighted in receiving Mercy! What's more, I wanted Mercy for my family and friends. Mercy was a Gift God offered. So I did *not* get to bump another out of the Mercy line because I didn't like him or the choices he made.

Resting on this tiny outcrop of revelation of God's Mercy, I was fortified. What comfort to understand that as long as we had breath, we had the opportunity to choose Jesus and receive His Mercy. Grander though was the Truth that *no one* was too far removed from God's Love. Second Peter 3:9, RSV, states, "The Lord is not slow about His promise as some count slowness, but is forbearing toward you, not wishing that *any* should perish, but that all should reach repentance," (emphasis mine).

Yet, as I continued upward, I was confronted with my own narrow-mindedness. As I struggled to climb this mountain, questions continued to assail me. Did the wicked go unpunished? Who is actually allowed in Heaven? The Holy Spirit revealed that while God's Love is for all, His Mercy is reserved for those who repent, turn from wickedness, and receive Jesus as their Savior and Lord. The two thieves nailed to crosses next to the Lord Jesus came to mind. One remained proud, spewing venom. The other was contrite, humbled, and used his last strength to honor Christ. Jesus covered that man with Mercy, promising him a place in Heaven.

Both these criminals, by the laws of their day, deserved to be crucified. Yet, one was promised the grandeur of Heaven. I, too, had been guilty of sin and deserved death, but I had asked Jesus for Mercy. He gave it. With that same measure, I now needed to give back to others. Luke recorded Jesus as teaching:

> "Do not judge, and you will not be judged. Do not condemn, and you will not be condemned. Forgive, and you will be forgiven. Give, and it will be given to you. A good measure, pressed down, shaken together and running over, will be poured into your lap. For with the measure you use, it will be measured to you," Luke 6:37-38, NIV.

I could not pile on the judgments and condemnation and expect that not to return to me in generous portions. I wanted forgiveness and mercy in heaps, so I had to give it in heaps! It was never mine to judge who was allowed in Heaven. Those in Heaven had humbly asked for Jesus, the True Judge, to be their Lord. Those in Heaven had repented of their sins.

Conversely, the thief on the cross that remained hard-hearted and proud was destined for Hell. Revelation 21:8 (NKJV) satisfied me, "But the cowardly, unbelieving, abominable, murderers, sexually immoral, sorcerers, idolaters, and all liars shall have their part in the lake which burns with fire and brimstone, which is the second death." Prideful and rebellious people were not given a get-out-of-jail-free card by God.

Yet, the impending question of Justice still loomed ahead. What did *God's* Justice look like? I had been experiencing a repeated dream, in which I was in a university, sheltering my slight friend with my arm, as I sought out something in the library. A professor heard my request, but instead of assisting me, he scolded me. Then he commanded we leave. We exited against the crush of students rushing to class. Frustrated, I guided my frail friend outside the library. The dream stopped there.

Upon awakening each time, I was disheartened. It seemed I could never find what I sought. And who was my companion? Why was she was so needy? After praying and seeking Godly insight, I gleaned some deeper understanding.

The university setting was human wisdom. The crush of students represented human thinking and pride. I was truly looking for something, but the professor—the authority of man—was telling me that I would not find what I was looking for there. As for the wisp of a girl, she was a very skewed, even erroneous, image of

Justice. One that revealed my belief that Justice was fragile—which was a distortion of God's Truth.

By reading God's Word, I came to see that God values Justice so much that He sits upon it daily. Psalm 89:14, NIV, says, "Righteousness and justice are the foundation of your throne; love and faithfulness go before you." Imagine how expansive and grand the foundations of His Throne must be! Justice is always in God's heart towards mankind.

Still, I stumbled on this mountain. How could I trust Justice when humankind had failed me so often?

Again, the answer was in God's Word, the Bible. Acts 17:31, NIV, states, "For he [God the Father] has set a day when he will judge the world with justice by the man [Jesus] he has appointed. He had given proof of this to everyone by raising him from the dead." When that day arrives, each of us will stand before a Holy God to give an account of our lives—each word, each act, and each motive (Romans 14:12, NIV, paraphrased). Additionally, 2 Corinthians 5:10, NIV, states, "For we must all appear before the judgment seat of Christ, so that each of us may receive what is due us for the things done while in the body, whether good or bad."

Jesus was the just Judge of the world. He wasn't blind, nor did He show favoritism or prejudices. There were no loopholes or exceptions. Each of us would give an account.

Each of us.

While no human justice has ever been served on my brother's behalf here on Earth, God saw Richard and knew his fate. That the person who murdered Richard would stand before a Holy God without repenting of his sin...with the murder of an innocent child on his heart...was terrifying! Yet no one who deserved the punishment of Hell would escape.

Those realizations removed any desire I had for revenge or retribution. Unlike the girl in my dream, God's Justice was never frail nor did it need my protection. God's Justice was like Him: unshakable and massive.

Like the mountain I had just scaled.

He did it! He had guided me over those mountains of faith-crushers. Revelation 21:7 encouraged me to aim high, [God the Father speaking] "He who overcomes shall inherit all things, and I will be his God and he shall be My son," (NKJV). That was what I desired! I better understood God's design of us humans as being free-willed creatures, able to choose between life and death. His unconditional Love, His offer of Mercy, and His fulfillment of Justice satisfied my relentless questions. Like a calf at a new gate, I was ready to embrace life.

God was Good!

I discovered the answers to the hard mountain-questions by continual prayer and study of God's Word. It was not instantaneous, but over time, answers came. I scaled one mountain at a time by repeatedly asking the Holy Spirit to reveal Truth to me as I studied God's Word. There was never a single "aha" moment. These life-giving concepts came about as the result of daily study and relationship with the Holy Spirit. He in turn, showed me Jesus.

9

Goodness

CURRENT TIMES

Every good gift and every perfect gift is from above, and comes down from the Father of lights, with whom there is no variation or shadow of turning.

—James 1:17 (NKJV)

My brother's disappearance and the subsequent trauma have marked me. However, it has not destroyed me. Most of the changes have benefitted me, and hopefully others with whom I share my journey. Remember when I was sixteen and I discovered the promise in Romans 8:28? The NASB states, "And we know God causes all things to work together for good to those who love God, to those who are called according to His purpose." In the face of tragedy and trauma, that was a bold statement. You may have cocked your head and asked, "How? Why? How could she have the audacity to proclaim God's Goodness in the midst of the trauma she experienced? Why would she express God's Goodness in her life?"

The simple answer to both questions is that God is Good. When

Moses was leading the people of Israel through the desert, he cried out to be shown God's Glory. In response God said He would show Moses His Goodness. Yet, as God passed by Moses, He proclaimed His Character:

> Now the LORD descended in the cloud and stood with him [Moses] there, and proclaimed the name of the LORD. And the LORD passed before him and proclaimed, "The LORD, the LORD God, merciful and gracious, longsuffering, and abounding in goodness and truth, keeping mercy for thousands, forgiving iniquity and transgression and sin, by no means clearing the guilty, visiting the iniquity of the fathers upon the children and the children's children to the third and the fourth generation," Exodus 34:5-7, NKJV.

All these characteristics—Sovereignty, Creator, Mercy, Grace, Patience, Goodness, Truth, Forgiveness and Justice—combine to form God's Goodness. Then add to that, the knowledge that God never changes—He is the same yesterday, today, and tomorrow—and we can know God's Goodness is trustworthy.

Longing for answers in the aftermath of Richard's disappearance led me to longing for God. As I sought Him, I found Him. God showed His Goodness toward me by offering me salvation through Jesus. Then He showed me how to make Jesus my Lord.

Despite living for so long with the unknown of Richard's fate and the yearning for closure, I had found a contentedness in my faith. I didn't have to know the details or have earthly justice. What I did not know or understand, God did. I had full confidence in Him.

Richard's disappearance also led me to a deep understanding of the Holy Spirit.

Jesus came to me through the ministry of the Holy Spirit to bind up my broken heart; to save my crushed spirit; and to grant me self-discipline and soundness. (Psalm 147:3, Psalm 34:18 and 2 Timothy 1:7, all NIV, paraphrased). This brought me clear thinking, peaceful thoughts, redeemed memories, and a consecrated imagination, all of which brought me closer to understanding Christ Jesus. Fear had schemed to have me to dwell on the turmoil, suffering, and loss. Instead, the Holy Spirit led me to visions that brought understanding and insight. Those visions solidified in my heart what happened to Richard and Jesus' role in it all, which yielded peace.

I also came to understand the difference between what I sensed in the spirit realm and the psychics: The Holy Spirit, part of a triune God, led me. He is the Spirit of Truth. Conversely, the psychics were led by demons. Satan is a liar, so the demons could not speak Truth, only lies.

Part of my renewal process was inner healing and deliverance-ministry prayers. I highly recommend seeking those trained in Sozo healing prayers. These were specific prayers for clarity, healing, and freedom of my soul. The Holy Spirit led me to Truth about God in these prayers. I repented of believing lies about others, God, and myself and received God's Truth. Jesus summarized it: "The thief [Satan] does not come except to steal, and to kill, and to destroy. I have come that they may have life, and that they may have it more abundantly," (John 10:10, NKJV).

I admit that writing this book stirred latent sadness, so earlier this year I also sought the wisdom of a Christian counselor trained in helping trauma victims find closure. As we talked, her validations of my experiences allowed me to articulate long-quiet grief. From that healing process, I have come to understand how zealous God is to have me free of the pain and entanglements of trauma.

Now I am able to love the Lord with a whole heart! Gone is the huge, dark closet in my brain with a "Do Not Disturb" sign on the door.

The violent nature of Jesus' Death on the Cross demonstrated that a compassionate Father's heart broke with His beloved Son's sufferings. God understood my family's agony. He was empathetic to our suffering as He held, comforted, and restored us.

Not only had God *not* abandoned my family, He called us to comfort others in the measure we ourselves had been comforted.

> Blessed be the God and Father of our Lord Jesus Christ, the Father of mercies and God of all comfort, who comforts us in all our tribulation, that we may be able to comfort those who are in any trouble, with the comfort with which we ourselves are comforted by God. For as the sufferings of Christ abound in us, so our consolation also abounds through Christ, (2 Corinthians 1:3-5, NKJV).

God designed our lives to matter to others. We were not to remain silent victims, but to become kind, compassionate overcomers. My parents achieved this by continuing to advocate for laws protecting missing children. I now minister to those who suffer trauma. We all allowed the Holy Spirit to use our experiences to teach and mature us so that we, in turn, teach, guide, and comfort others with His Hope.

That is part of the Goodness He brought from our sufferings.

The Goodness of the Lord also displayed itself in the power of praying for others, or intercession. I am confident my family would have disintegrated in the aftermath of the trauma if it had not been for Christian intercession. I found a box stuffed with letters sent to my parents in the early years from people across the nation. Their prayers brought my parents comfort and strength. My parents kept those cards of support for the rest of their lives.

I learned to pray God's Word over situations or people. Intercession was, and is, a powerful tool to establish Peace and Justice. I have had the joy of praying with several people dear to my heart, as they received Jesus as their Savior and Lord. One of those persons was my father!

Like honey, the Goodness of God kept spreading, sticking to each heart.

* * *

While I grieve over our culture's gruesome fascination with violence and the glamorization of death, I also am confident in God's Love, Jesus' Victory, and the Comfort of the Holy Spirit. God was and is Sovereign, Almighty, and Good. And Just. I believe Heaven will include the Judgment Seat, on which Jesus will Judge all. In 2 Timothy 4:1, Paul tells us, "I charge you therefore before God and the Lord Jesus Christ, who will judge the living and the dead at His appearing and His kingdom...," (NKJV). Yet, God doesn't desire *any* to perish: His Good Heart is that all would follow Jesus to Heaven.

The wonders of Heaven were revealed to me in another vision. With Mercy, Jesus took me to a crowded, noisy Middle Eastern open-air market, with vendors offering their many wares. While the throng of peaceful people kept me from seeing more than two feet in front of me, Jesus strode ahead with long, even steps. Everyone, including Jesus, wore white linen robes and colorful sashes across their chests, tied at one hip. The sashes were different colors—gold, green, purple, blue, and more.

I was the only one dressed in western-styled blue jeans.

I walked fast to keep up, straining to hear Jesus's explanation for the sashes. He turned His head over His shoulder as He spoke, telling me each color represented some honorable quality of their character, such as mercy or compassion.

Suddenly, Jesus stopped in front of an orange vendor, who asked if I would like an orange. In a place deep inside me I remembered how Richard had devoured oranges as his favorite food.

"I don't have any money to purchase an orange," I said.

Then the vendor, a handsome man about thirty-years-old and wearing a turquoise sash, turned to me. He held an orange the size of a cantaloupe with both hands. His generous offer and gentle smile cut through me. He was so peaceful and kind.

Jesus explained it would be okay to take the orange because no one exchanged money here. They all simply gave away what they had. I nodded and thanked the merchant, who then gleamed while I peeled and tasted the orange, asking if the flavor was to my liking.

Jesus tenderly spoke. "You don't know who the vendor is, do you? It's Richard. He's here, in Heaven. He's grown into a man full of compassion and generosity. You may hug him if you like."

Immediately I was in my brother's arms! Tears of gratitude and joy flowed down my cheeks. We hugged. He pulled back and smiled brightly. Next, Jesus took my arm and said it was time to leave.

That vision remains one of my deepest treasures. It is as real to me as breathing. It brought depths of healing to my longing heart. What a compassionate God to give that to me!

* * *

Mom's death also held the promise of Heaven. In her final hours, a virulent strain of pneumonia made her struggle to breathe. Each breath was painful, though the medical team offered her palliative care in her final hours.

A loved one whispered in her ear, "Go. Go eat supper with your son in Heaven."

A single tear slipped out of Mom's eyes. Then she closed her eyes and seemed to rest. Suddenly her eyes flew open, grew big, and were illuminated with a Light none of us could see. The Light radiated in her eyes, yet it was not actually visible to us in the room. Mom gasped, smiled, and then passed on.

It was so peaceful!

* * *

Dad and I had always delighted in one another's company, but more so after Mom passed. He continued to be creative, opinionated, caring, and funny. He attended church on a regular basis, but was unsure of his salvation. At the age of 87, I had the honor of leading my beloved dad to the Savior and Lord Jesus Christ, Who, in turn, was faithful to Dad's prayers to the very end of his natural life. I treasure that!

* * *

Over time, God has healed the open, gaping wounds in my soul. I no longer need the answers humans provide. The yearning for closure was satisfied, no longer a threat to my peace of mind, nor my happiness. God was and is the answer to a longing unfulfilled or a need unmet. All the restlessness and striving that had beset me in the years following Richard's disappearance has been stilled. Where there was once disquiet and yearning, Jesus has established freedom, comfort, and hope.

I can declare the Goodness of the Lord Jesus in my life! I am confident that God establishes His Goodness in all situations. Whatever you face today, may you put your trust in Him and see what He has in store for you. Have faith. Believe the promise of His ability to bring Good.

Recently I had another vision—this time of myself speaking in a church setting. Afterwards, a man presented me with a copper bracelet engraved with my brother's name and the date of his disappearance on the shiny surface, much like the POW/MIA bracelets in the 1970s. He held it out as a warm gift.

I held his gaze, tilting my head to one side. "No, thank you. You see, my brother is not missing. He is in the Presence of our Lord Jesus, the King. And truly, he was never missing from Him Who Sees All. He was never missing from Him Who Matters Most. God is Omniscient, Omnipresent, and Omnipotent. I don't need such a bracelet. I have Peace."

God is Good.

PRAYER FOR READERS

If you gathered any Hope or feel a pull on your heart—if you want Peace, please read this prayer out loud to God the Father. May Goodness and Mercy be yours.

Heavenly Father,

    You are kind, gracious, slow to anger, and always good. I want to honor you. Please forgive me when I chose myself over You. Please forgive me for being afraid. Please forgive my sins against You. May Your Son, Jesus, who came in the flesh and lived and died for me now come live in my heart as my Savior and Lord. I give Him my past, my hurts, my struggles, my sins, as well as my future.

    Jesus, You took all this upon Yourself at the Cross. You rose, conquering fear and death. You carried my sorrows, sickness, and sin. You are the Risen Lord!

    Thank You that You long to be gracious to me. As I turn my life over to You, I believe You will bring Good out of the tragedies and injustices that have beset me in the past. In places of pain, I receive Your Hope and Peace. You are my Comfort.

I want to know You, Jesus, as a King of Justice. I want to know Your Goodness. Thank You for helping and guiding me. Thank You for strengthening me and granting me Your Peace. Thank You for singing songs of deliverance over me. I trust You, even when it doesn't make sense. I rest in You, Jesus.

In Jesus' Holy Name, Amen.

NOTES

CHAPTER 3: Terror

1. Kaston, Richard O., "Did Richard Griener Reach Sledding Hill?" *Journal Star*, (Peoria, IL), Feb. 12, 1972, AM, B-12.

2. "Pekin Boy, 13, Still Missing; Mass Search Conducted E. of Pekin," *Pekin Daily Times*, (Pekin, IL), Jan. 18, 1972, 1.

3. *Ibid.*

4. "Story of A Search; Boy is Still Missing," *Pekin Daily Times*, (Pekin, IL), Jan. 19, 1972, 2.

5. "Pekin Boy, 13, Still Missing; Search to Resume Today" *Journal Star*, (Peoria, IL), Jan. 19, 1972, AM, D-16.

CHAPTER 4: Chaos

1. "Story of a Search; Boy Is Still Missing," *Pekin Daily Times*, (Pekin, IL), Jan. 19, 1972, 2.

2. "Pekin Boy, 13, Still Missing; Search to Resume Today," *Journal Star*, (Peoria, IL), Jan. 19, 1972, AM, D-16.

3. "Pekin Police Intensify Search For Clues of Missing Boy," *Journal Star*, (Peoria, IL), Jan. 19, 1972, PM, D-16.

4. "No New Leads; Pekin Boy Is Still Missing," *Pekin Daily Times*, (Pekin, IL), Jan. 20, 1972, 2.

5. "Mother Certain Boy Didn't Run Away; Left Items Home," *Journal Star*, (Peoria, IL), PM, Jan. 20, 1972, B-1.

6. "No New Leads; Pekin Boy Is Still Missing," *Pekin Daily Times*, (Pekin, IL), Jan. 20, 1972, 2.

7. Kaston, Richard O., "'Lead' That Failed in Griener Case; Mystery Youth Was Wrong Boy," *Journal Star*, (Peoria, IL), PM, Feb. 7, 1972, B-12.

8. *Ibid.*

9. Kaston, Richard O., "Did Richard Griener Reach Sledding Hill?" *Journal Star*, (Peoria, IL), Feb. 12, 1972, AM, B-12.

10. "Disappearance of Illinois 13-Year-Old Baffles Police," *Springfield Daily News*, (Springfield, MO), Feb. 23, 1972, 5.

CHAPTER 5: Normalcy

1. "Pekin Boy, 9, Missing Since Last Friday," *Pekin Daily Times*, (Pekin, IL), Aug. 3, 1976, 2.

2. "Pekin Boy's Body Found In Boxcar In East Peoria," *Journal Star*, (Peoria, IL), PM, Aug. 24, 1976, A-1.

3. Barnard, Marge, "Fairground Drifter Suspected in the Slaying of Mark Helmig, But No Charges To Be Filed Here," *Pekin Daily Times*, (Pekin, IL), Aug. 21, 1979, 1.

4. Yung, Bernie, "Guatney Recalls 1976 Tazewell 4-H Fair," *Journal Star*, (Peoria, IL), PM, Aug. 22, 1979, D-16.

5. "Guatney Early Suspect," *Journal Star*, (Peoria, IL), PM, Aug. 22, 1979, D-16.

6. Adams, Pam, "Father of Missing Pekin Boy Without Hope; Body Found in Normal Not Richard Griener's," *Journal Star*, (Peoria, IL), PM, July 17, 1978, C-16.

7. "Griener Dental Records To Be Sent To Chicago," *Journal Star*, (Peoria, IL), AM, Dec. 28, 1978, D-16.

8. "Police To Dig Up Gacy Yard; First Body Identified," *Journal Star*, (Peoria, IL), AM, Dec. 31, 1978, A-2.

9. "State Rests Case Against John Gacy," *Journal Star*, (Peoria, IL), PM, Feb. 21, 1980, A-2.

10. "Police To Dig Up Gacy Yard; First Body Identified," *Journal Star*, (Peoria, IL), AM, Dec. 31, 1978, A-2.

11. Barnard, Marge, "Fairground Drifter Suspected in Slaying of Mark Helmig, But No Charges To Be Filed Here," *Pekin Daily Times*, (Pekin, IL), Aug. 21, 1979, 1.

12. *Ibid.*

13. Simpson, Kevin, "Suspect in '79 Case Has Died in Kansas," *Pantograph*, (Bloomington, IL), April 4, 1997, 5, https://www.newspapers.com/clip/1650959/4041997/, accessed October 14, 2020.

CHAPTER 7: Forgiveness

1. Young, William, P., *The Shack*, Newbury Park, CA: Windblown Media, 2007.

2. Zemeckis, Robert. 1994. *Forrest Gump*. United States: Paramount Pictures.

3. www.NamUs.gov, accessed 17. Nov. 2020.

4. Rumore, Kori and Kyle Bentle, "Chicago History: Here Are John Gacy's Victims," https://www.chicagotribune.com/history/ct-john-wayne-gacy-victims-20181215-htmlstory.html. Dec. 28, 2018, 8:58 AM, accessed Nov. 28, 2020.

ACKNOWLEDGMENTS

I wish to thank following people, each of whom contributed to the completion of this memoir:

My fifth-grade substitute teacher who sheltered me; Larry and Linda, who first ministered Jesus Christ to me; Franci, who gently nudged me to share more; Farley, who encouraged me that the story was worth telling; Andrea, whose zeal for life strengthens me; Kerry, who inspires me to love others well; Trudi, who lives with joy, freedom, justice, and truth; Katy and the Prisoner of Hope team—your zealous love of Jesus brings Truth; my faithful intercessors—Anne, Jane, Joyce, Meghann, Paula, Sandy, and Tonya—you love well; Detective Henry Rush III of Midwest Protective Services, Inc., who was the first to advocate for Richard and to validate my family's experiences; Alana, whose compassion allowed much healing; writing coach Karen Ball, who helped me articulate deep pain; and Sandra, who continues to sharpen my faith.

Thank you all for believing the memoir was worth telling. Your expertise, prayers, and kindness were invaluable to me.

POSTSCRIPT

Not all the suspects in my brother's disappearance are referenced in this memoir. Since no one was ever charged with the crime, it seemed unnecessary to delve into each and every one.